17.06.07.

To Neil and Clare,
With thanks and best wishes,
Love from all at All Saints

HIGH WYCOMBE
PAST

The High Street in the 1890s.

HIGH WYCOMBE PAST

James Rattue

Phillimore

2002

Published by
PHILLIMORE & CO. LTD
Shopwyke Manor Barn, Chichester, West Sussex

ISBN 1 86077 218 8

Printed and bound in Great Britain by
BIDDLES LTD
Guildford, Surrey

Contents

List of Illustrations

Frontispiece: The High Street in the 1890s

Illustration Acknowledgements

Many thanks to the following who have given permission for the publication of photographs and images: High Wycombe Library, 2, 3, 9, 27, 68, 74, 76, 79, 80, 88, 100, 146; The *Bucks Free Press*, 33, 77, 90, 81, 83, 87, 101, 108, 114, 115, 119, 120, 122, 124, 137, 145; the High Wycombe Society, 10, 99, 130, 132, 135, 139, 147; Bucks County Museum, 13, 55, 102; Mr D.A. Cornwall, 17, 20, 72; Mr and Mrs A. Colmer, 20, 37; the Churchwardens of St Mary and St George's church, Sands, 104, 106. All these people and institutions have lent me their pictures for no charge, for which I am most grateful. All other images come from the Museum collection. Corinna Whitfield took nos. 136 and 140 and and Robert Hoare reproduced many of the pictures specially for this book.

Acknowledgements

I am very much in the debt of Wycombe's previous historians, L.J. Ashford and John Mayes—Chapter Two is particularly based on Ashford's book—and the pages of the *Bucks Free Press* have formed a major source for Wycombe's more recent history. Other works consulted are listed in the Bibliography, and Wycombe Museum's files and oral history recordings have also proved invaluable: I am grateful for the help and comments of Mrs Inez Wright, Mr Ash Chaudhri and Mr Norman Timpson in this respect. A fully annotated copy of the text will be kept at the Museum in case references are required.

Thanks are further due to Wycombe District Council for giving me the opportunity to write this book, to Mr Ian Horwood and Mr Martin Rickards for checking the text, to the Council's Economic Development staff for help and advice, and to all the many inhabitants of High Wycombe who have contributed towards this new view of their town's history.

One

'Valley with a Stream'
(up to 1226)

In 1878 John Parker, former Town Clerk and local antiquarian, summed up the early growth of High Wycombe in the phrase 'the stream made the mills, the mills the market and the market the town'. The stream he referred to, which is universally known today as the Wye, was not even named until the 1810s, when military map-makers assumed that the name 'Wycombe' contained the title of the river; but Parker had made a valuable point. The river, cutting a valley through the otherwise dry Chiltern hills and linking the Thames with the ancient Icknield Way that ran along the foot of the chalk escarpment, did indeed provide three crucial factors behind Wycombe's growth: water, an important routeway, and power. It made the valley an ideal place for people to settle.

As well as being favoured by nature, the confluence of the Wycombe and Hughenden streams seems to have been 'significant' in some peculiar way for the area's early settlers. In addition to leaving the first evidence of human activity in the Wye Valley in the form of flint axes and arrowheads, the Neolithic people may also have left us traces of a sacred landscape. Beneath the north wall of the parish church is a sarsen boulder brought here by glacial floodwaters and, despite looking completely out of place, it has remained unmoved through several rebuildings. Another mysterious stone stands outside the Guildhall, although its modern name—the Dog Stone—does not imply any

great surviving reverence for it! Finally, the Gosspring Stone once stood at the north end of Frogmoor as one of the boundary marks of the ancient borough. These stones could be the remains of a stone circle or other megalithic monument. Marking the eastern edge of the borough and the boundary of the Rye was the Holy Well, first alluded to in the 1170s as one of a number of springs whose superstitious rituals were condemned by Bishop Hugh of Lincoln. It was probably a site of reverence for thousands of years before being recorded, and only disappeared when the swimming pool was built in the 1950s. These clues are too fragmentary to give a clear picture, but they hint at a special importance for the Wye Valley.

In time, this 'significant place' was marked with earthworks on the hilltops. Desborough Castle to the west was an Iron-Age hillfort based on the site of a much older Bronze-Age henge. When the system of Anglo-Saxon administrative units called 'hundreds' was established and Wycombe found itself at the centre of Desborough Hundred, the site of the 'hundred moot' where trials and other legal business were conducted was probably close by. It was only reasonable that 18th-century antiquarians should assume that Desborough Castle was the location of the moot; but the name was only given to the hillfort in the mid-1700s and its most common local name was 'The Roundabout', so the moot was probably held elsewhere. Another henge topped Church

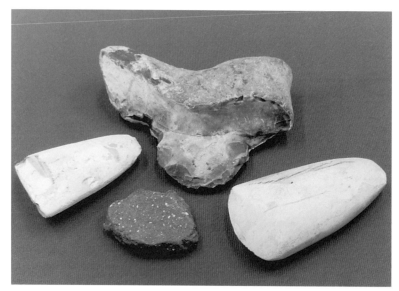

1 Fragments of an ancient past: a Neolithic hand-held flint chopper and a potsherd found in Frogmoor in 1972; part of a polished flint axe-head from Fassets Road, Loudwater; and a complete axe-head found in Carrington Road.

2 'Roundabout Wood', marking the site of Desborough Castle, in 1922. There has only ever been partial excavation of this ancient monument, now incongruously surrounded by the estates of Castlefield. The monument is viewed from the east: Copyground Farm is in the dip on the right.

3   The Rye's Roman villa, with its bath-house and outbuildings, was excavated three times in all. This is the 1932 dig organised by Francis Colmer with the advice of archaeological celebrity Sir Mortimer Wheeler. Funds for a full excavation were not available and the site had to wait until the Ministry of Works examined it in 1954.

Hill, West Wycombe, overlooking the headwaters of the river. Here, legend relates, the villagers finally built their church after the Devil transported the stones there at night from the original site at the foot of the hill! This story is told in many places and folklorists believe it to be a coded account of a church being moved to a site of pagan worship. Totteridge, too, may have had a 'Castle'; Malmer's Well, a 'British Camp' to the north of Castle Hill, was still visible in the 1700s; and on Keep Hill, to the south, there are earthworks where in 1826 labourers discovered 11 gold Celtic coins inside a hollow flint.

Remnants of Roman Wycombe never completely disappeared—thin Roman bricks can be seen in the tower of the church and in St John's Hospital on Easton Street—but this period in the town's history really came to light only in 1724 when workmen uncovered a mosaic pavement on Great Penns Mead beside the Rye. The site was excavated in 1863, 1932

and 1954, and these digs revealed a large villa with a complex bathhouse, built around A.D. 150 and abandoned in the mid-fourth century. In fact, the villa is another clue suggesting the special nature of the Wye Valley: it stood in close proximity to the Holy Well spring whose waters very probably supplied its baths, a relationship which can be found between Roman sites and sacred springs elsewhere in the country. But the villa did not stand in an empty landscape. Roman remains have been found all along the valley, from a well near the Priory in Castle Street, discovered about 1870, to pottery fragments unearthed during work on the High Street in 1998, along with possible buildings at Hughenden and Micklefield. The villa may have been the centre of a large estate with several outlying farms.

The area seems to have followed this pattern for several centuries. The first record of the place-name 'Wycombe' is often said to have come in 800 when an army of the Kingdom of

4 The interior of the parish church, drawn by E.J. Niemann in the 1840s, before the refurbishment according to the principles of the Ecclesiological Movement. This involved removing the box pews, the candelabra, the pulpit with its sounding-board, the Royal Arms, and the Carrington Pew over the chancel arch, which went to the Abbey hall.

Mercia marched through 'Wiecum', but this is a Tudor chronicler's mistake: the actual route went through a different place entirely, located in Gloucestershire. Instead the first documentary record of High Wycombe's existence came in about 970. *Wicumun*—probably meaning '(the place in) the valley with a stream'—is a plural word, indicating a string of settlements along the valley. These included Croynden (which gave its name to Crendon Street) and Horsenden on the Marlow Hill side. Together, without yet constituting anything like a town, these hamlets made up what was listed in Domesday Book in 1086 as the ninth wealthiest manor in Buckinghamshire, owned by the Crown.

The church was a key institution in early Wycombe. All the clues are there to suggest that All Saints was originally a 'minster', acting as a base for a group of priests who served the surrounding villages before they had churches of their own: it was built in a pagan place, in the centre of a wealthy royal manor, and close to a meeting-place of the hundred, as well as being unusually large. On the other hand, the legend of St Walstan, Bishop of Worcester, relates that he consecrated Wycombe's church in the 1070s or 1080s at the behest of a local lord. This suggests that it was simply a manorial church of the sort which were being founded all across the country—if a big one. In those early years, the existence of the church would have encouraged settlement to concentrate around it, but it would never be quite as important in Wycombe's history again. In other towns where the merchants remained subject to the lord of the manor, such as Chesham, religious guilds and fraternities, which paid for Mass to be said for the souls of their departed members, provided an outlet for their energies and became rather like surrogate local councils. Wycombe was fortunate enough to develop the real thing, and its Guild of St Mary stuck to religious purposes despite including most of the leading citizens in the Middle Ages.

At this point the river became crucial once more, powering the mills which began to grow up along the valley. Domesday Book recorded six mills in the Manor of Wycombe. Ash, Bridge and Pann Mills, equally spaced around the old Borough, probably represent three of these as they were all named in records before 1200; and the other three could be Marsh, Loudwater and Hedge Mills further down the valley. Temple and Bassetsbury Mills were probably built after the splitting-up of the Manor in 1203 so that each estate had a mill more conveniently placed. As the 13th century wore on these were joined by Rye and Bowden's Mills which, together with more in the parishes of West Wycombe and Wooburn, made the so-called Wye a 'busy little river' indeed.

The produce of the mills had to be sold, and, in common with many Anglo-Saxon towns, the market place developed at the churchyard gate. The market possibly existed as early as the 1100s, when the lord of the manor supposedly collected taxes from it. Probably in the 1150s or 1160s, the Crown decided to encourage trade by laying out the High Street with long, narrow 'burgage plots' fronting onto it, and the 'burgesses' who owned them were another distinctive mark of a borough town. Over the same period the Manor was divided. At first small portions along the valley were detached; in about 1175 Henry II granted the Wycombe Rectory lands to Godstow Abbey in Oxford; and finally in 1203 King John divided what remained into two parts, the area south and west of the High Street which became Temple Wycombe, and the estate based on the house later called Bassetsbury. The developing 'borough' lay mainly within the latter, and the burgesses were subject to the charges of the lord of the manor.

Over the decades this situation clearly began to frustrate the burgesses. Their entrepreneurship was filling the coffers at Bassetsbury with no obvious benefit to themselves; and they

5 Mr Jarvis in Pann Mill in the 1950s. The Jarvises had been operating the mill since Robert Jarvis moved in during the late 1920s.

6 The heart of the town: stalls in Wycombe Market, photographed from the Guildhall in 1998. One of the key institutions of Wycombe's history, the market has survived over 900 years despite its ups and downs.

7 The Rye painted by Annie Giles about 1887, with Bassetsbury Manor and Barn in the background. The Rye is now Wycombe's 'green lung', but for many centuries it had an equally vital function as the town's common pastureland, where every burgess had the right to graze cattle. It marks the eastern edge of the ancient borough.

8 The Cattle Market had moved from Cornmarket to Frogmoor in 1907, but this photograph can only date from after 1913 to judge by the poster advertising the Grand Cinema, so the docile cow is a little out of place. It may be a stray from one of the dairy herds.

were in a good position to hear about the advantages that independent borough status had brought other towns. By the 1220s the Abbess of Godstow, supported by the burgesses, was taking the lord, Alan Basset, to court to challenge his right to levy rents on the houses built in the parts of the town she owned. One particular complaint was that the householders piled up dung from their animals in front of their houses ready to spread on their landholdings around the town, only to find

that Basset's men were gathering it up to spread on his fields! After the abbess and Basset came to terms, the burgesses argued on and (although he retained his rights to the dung) in 1226 the lord of the manor agreed to demise 'the whole borough of Wycombe, with its rents, markets and fairs' to the burgesses for an annual rent of £30 and a mark. For the first time, the borough had explicit legal recognition, and the burgesses acting together were the main authority in the town. Wycombe had become independent.

Two

Market Borough
(1226–1880)

Twenty-six burgesses signed as witnesses the agreement liberating the town from the lord of the manor. How a man became a 'burgess', with all the privileges it entailed—trading without being taxed, and participating in making local laws—is not clear. Presumably it originally involved owning one of the burgage plots along the main streets, although the right later became hereditary. Unfortunately few early Wycombe records survive, and when the town's Ledger Book was compiled in 1475 no documents earlier than 1309 were copied into it. However, those first entries in the Book show the borough as a body going to court, holding its own courts, and making by-laws, and it prob-

ably did so from the very beginning. Certainly the first document bearing the borough seal—a guarantee that the will of one Adam Walder would be carried out—dates to within a few years of the fateful agreement of 1226.

The town would carry on paying its annual fee-farm 'rent' to the lord of the manor for centuries, but after the last resident member of the Bassett family, Philip, died in 1271, the lack of a lord living on their doorsteps left the burgesses free to go their own way. Bassetsbury fell into the hands of the Crown in 1326, and moved in and out of them before being granted to the Dean and Chapter of St George's Chapel, Windsor, in 1483. They let it to a succession

9 Bassetsbury Manor being renovated. Fred Skull, local antique dealer and member of a furniture-making dynasty, bought the house in 1931 and spent a small fortune converting the ruinous old Manor into a period home, clearing out the apartments and building a new wing.

10 The Old Post Office, Easton Street. Currently Rigs Wine Bar, the story goes that this was originally a dower house of the Dashwoods; there is no direct proof of this, but its style does resemble buildings on the West Wycombe estate. Parker's solicitors occupied it, then it housed the Post Office until the move to Queen Victoria Road in 1934.

of tenants (including the Dashwoods of West Wycombe in the 1700s), some of whom attempted to take part in local affairs, and some of whom did not; the manor house was subjected to the indignity of use as farm buildings, then housed the Lancasterian School (1812-28), and was eventually split into inadequate and insanitary apartments. In the 1870s the Church Commissioners acquired the estate, and finally sold it off in bits in 1882, liberating such properties as Loudwater Mills and Totteridge House. At any rate, the lords and the tenants of Bassetsbury were usually in no position to interfere with the development of the nascent borough.

Wycombe's first public officials were its two Bailiffs followed later by the Gildans who dealt with the affairs of the merchant gild to which all burgesses also belonged. The first

Mayor, Roger Outred, was appointed some time between 1276 and 1286. Although only a small proportion of the young town's people were burgesses, for them the early borough was an egalitarian institution. In the early 14th century the legislative body was described as 'the whole community in full Gild Hall' and by 1477 the town's 'law days' were held on the Rye, still with all the burgesses attending. By that time, nevertheless, some had become more important than others. In 1432 the mayor and six other burgesses signed a lease of a property in Crendon Lane on behalf of the whole borough; two of the six had represented Wycombe in Parliament and three had been mayor, so these were among the wealthiest and most prominent men in the town. This happened more and more often over the next fifty years, until Wycombe was effectively governed by an 'executive committee' who acted 'with the counsel, consent, wish and assent of all the other burgesses'. In 1498 it was decided that before a burgess was put forward as mayor he should first have served in this body, the 'Counsaille Howse', whose members were the 'Mayor's brethren', elected by the whole of the burgesses. In 1511 they were called aldermen for the first time.

It was a far bigger step to remove the democratic element completely. In 1558 Wycombe received its first formal charter, which failed to mention the law days, or the Borough Court in which every burgess sat. Queen Elizabeth's charter of 1598 constituted the mayor and aldermen as a 'Common Council'; and finally in 1609 a third charter placed the election of new aldermen in the hands of the existing ones. As a result, the council became an entirely self-perpetuating body, elected by themselves and answerable only to themselves. The only outbreak of democracy for the next 250 years came in 1721 when all the burgesses were consulted to depose Edward Bedder from the mayoralty after he 'elected' burgesses without authority.

The core of the Common Council's business was, then as it had always been, managing the market. Just west of the church, in the huge original market place, a Gild Hall was built in the early 1300s. It was not demolished until 1930, although it had been partly superseded by the 'Market House' on the south side of corn market in the late 1400s; this second building, itself rebuilt in 1604 and again in 1757, became referred to as the Guild Hall in the early 1900s. In an age when cash was scarce and there was little point in travelling to villages to trade, markets were economically vital and to control one was a powerful asset. The council's chief responsibility was to ensure that buyers were not cheated, and consequently it kept standard measures to check the produce being sold. In 1673 the mayor was indicted at the County Sessions for not keeping a standard bushel, while in 1703 the council ordered that

the 'toll dishes' in which the tolls of grain were collected should be 'gaged by the standard and sealed with the Towne Seale'. The council also enforced laws against the ancient market crimes of forestalling (trading before the market bell had sounded) and regrating (buying to sell on at a profit), and made sure that no one evaded its tolls and charges on traders who were not burgesses. Most important of these levies was the corn toll, the mainstay of the borough's finances just as the corn market was the engine of the local economy. At first it was paid to the mayor for his expenses, and his share was fixed at £50 in 1660; by 1781 it was raising £277 and was paying for all sorts of things, including a House of Correction which received prisoners from a considerable area around the town. The local importance of the market was demonstrated in 1665 when the council complained that people were coming from as far afield as Wendover, Amersham and Weston Underwood and trying to sell grain without paying the tolls.

11 The tollhouse on Amersham Road at Terriers. This thoroughfare was laid out as a turnpike road in 1768. The plaque was dated 1883—not to mark when the tollhouse was built (it was much older), but when it was acquired by the Carrington estate, as indicated by the estate's cypher, the three linked 'C's.

Regulations were relaxed for the great annual fairs; in 1564, for instance, shoemakers from outside Wycombe were allowed to sell their wares in the town, but only on fair days. St Margaret's Fair, held in support of the leper hospital, began in the 1220s, and from 1239 St John's Hospital had a fair in Easton Street on St Thomas's Day; but it was the Michaelmas cattle fair which was the main event. Alan Basset had had a cattle fair on Bassetsbury land before he came to terms with the burgesses, and this eventually moved to the High Street under the aegis of the borough. By the mid-1800s—and probably much earlier—it had become partly a 'hiring fair' at which boys, girls and men seeking work for the coming season, mainly in agricultural trades, would gather to be hired by

the farmers. The fair was thus an enormously important institution in the life of the whole area.

But Wycombe was not an ordinary market town. London was only twenty-odd miles away to the east, and Oxford lay a similar distance westwards. Wycombe occupied a most convenient point to break the journey between the two. The road also included Windsor Castle and the medieval royal palace at Woodstock, and indeed in 1170 Henry II levied a charge on the Manor of Wycombe for moving his silverware from the former to the latter. This road, leading straight to the capital's corn market at Newgate, appeared on Gough's map of 1335, and in 1351 a London corn dealer, Walter Neal, left a bequest for its repair. Institutions to look

12 This well-known print of the High Street made in 1772 by William Hannan shows the broad thoroughfare of a proud and prosperous market town, following the same line as its medieval original—'the longest, widest, and finest street in Buckinghamshire', claimed Joseph Sheahan in 1862. Each person shown was an identifiable local character.

after travellers grew up in the town, from the religious—St John's Hospital on Easton Street—to the secular, such as the *Newynne* and the *Sarasenhede* mentioned in 1312 (one of the first inhabitants of the town whose name we know was, in fact, Nicholas 'le Vinetur', a 13th-century innkeeper). Originally the main route followed the valley along the Thames from Windsor and Maidenhead and then ran beside the Wye, curving into Wycombe via what became St Mary Street, and arriving at all the important places—Bridge Mill, the market place, the Guildhall and the church. Converging on the market place were the streets lined with the houses of the burgesses and other townspeople, and, increasingly, the taverns and inns catering for travellers.

Gradually the direct road to London, with all its business and society traffic, overshadowed the old royal route to Windsor. In 1681 the Earl of Shaftesbury, on his way to Parliament

13 St John's Hospital on London Road was an important organisation in the medieval town and its Mastership was a key position; after the hospital's dissolution in the 1530s its revenues were used to support the Grammar School. The campaign to save the ruins was led by antiquarian Francis Colmer, who drew this sketch in 1930.

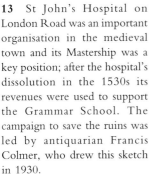

14 Houses on Oxford Road which later became the *King's Head* inn, from a sketch made in 1784 and then copied in 1810. This is one of the earliest depictions of buildings in the town and nicely shows the river Wye running along the roadside.

15 This 1920s view shows the grotto and cascades constructed along a backwater of the Wye known as the Dyke as part of the landscaping of the Loakes grounds allegedly carried out by Capability Brown in the 1760s. At the same time, the main Maidenhead road was diverted from its old course to run north of the Rye.

16 The old St Mary Street, looking towards Bridge Mill and photographed about 1940. The street was the ancient route into Wycombe, and in the Middle Ages contained the homes of wealthy burgesses. Centuries later it included some of the worst housing in the town.

17 *Left.* This mysterious medieval barn stood behind the buildings of Church Street and White Hart Street, and was identified as the remnants of Wycombe's first Guildhall in the 1920s. It was superseded by the 'Market House' on the south side of Cornmarket in the 1400s. Francis Colmer drew it in 1928, a couple of years before it was demolished.

18 *Below.* Coaching traffic. The main pubs along High Wycombe High Street for centuries were stopping-points for the coaching trade. The 'Tetsworth Flyer', shown here, and other coaches carried on visiting the *Falcon Hotel* until the early 1900s.

19 *Right.* Castle Street from the corner with Priory Road in about 1900. The Priory (a 16th-century house said, on little evidence, to have belonged to the Abbess of Godstow) is on the left, followed by Chantry House, the three-storey Town House, and the angled front of the Vicarage, demolished in 1964.

at Oxford, stated that 'the road was so full of coaches that there was going down Stokenchurch hill fourteen coaches and I believe thirty horse at one time'. A Turnpike Trust for the section from Beaconsfield to Stokenchurch was set up in 1718 to levy tolls on vehicles and improve the road; and the council had no objections when, in 1762, Lord Shelburne offered to divert the old road running south of the Rye to the north—and away from his gardens. To give some idea of the wealth the road was capable of bringing to Wycombe, the rent for the right to collect the turnpike tolls rose from £362 in 1724 to £3,500 in 1837.

Proximity to London had other effects too. For centuries before the chair industry developed, the Chiltern woodlands supplied fuel for the metropolis (in 1218, for instance, 14,000 bundles of wood were sent from West Wycombe to Southwark), and the presence of London grain dealers in Wycombe's market place helped to push prices there above the general level in the region. In the 13th century, Wycombe became a chief supplier of bread to

the royal court at Westminster, beginning with an order for 8,000 loaves for the Christmas feast in 1241. This coincided with the Manor of Wycombe falling temporarily into the hands of the Crown on the death of Gilbert Basset, but the Court kept the orders coming for forty years. In Christmas 1245 the order was for £10-worth of bread, as much as was requested from London itself.

But the most important single trade in the medieval and Tudor town, and yet again one which was supplying metropolitan needs, was cloth manufacture. Linen and hemp cloth was more important locally than wool: when the Abbess of Godstow leased out the rectory of Wycombe in the late 1200s, she was careful to keep the tithes on linen and hemp for her abbey. Several of the Wye mills were fitted with fulling hammers to pound the cloth, shrinking and strengthening it, including Hedge Mill (mentioned as Hochedsmill in 1411), an unnamed mill on the Rye in the early 1600s, and probably Glory and Cores End mills in Wooburn and Bourne End. By 1250, the clothmakers were already powerful enough to make sure that when a new fulling mill was built in Loudwater it would not use cloth made in the borough, and so divert trade away from the existing mills. In 1511 there were enough

of them to be organised under the control of their 'wardens'. By 1623 the industry was said to be 'much decayed', but the council still made efforts to support it: in 1630 it debated the case of a 'foreign' dyer, Daniel Stockwell, discovered selling his wares in the market, and ordered that 'no forraine dier shall come to make benefitt of his trade'.

Contacts with London were on a personal as well as an economic level, with a constant traffic of people to and fro. Perhaps the most notable medieval example was William Redhode, whose family came from the capital to Wycombe before 1414. William then moved back again and made his fortune as a salter, before returning to his native town to become its mayor, and donated the Ledger Book to the borough to mark his mayoralty in 1475. Wycombe continued to attract settlers brought in by the Oxford-to-London road, setting it apart from other towns. In 1851 fully 38 per cent of the adult population had been born more than five miles away, as opposed to 31 per cent in Marlow and only 27 per cent in sleepy Princes Risborough. This pattern carried on into the 20th century.

But Wycombe's geographical position did not always work to its advantage; during the Civil War of the 1640s, when the town was

20 The 18th-century Fryer's Mill in Fryer's Lane, depicted in its dereliction by Francis Colmer in about 1940.

21 The decisions of the borough authorities were written in the Ledger Book from 1475 onwards. Mayor William Redhode paid for it to be made, and it still survives in the borough archives.

22 Emily Strange, a lace-maker, was born in 1845 and was married to William, a Stokenchurch chair-maker. This photograph shows her at the Almshouses in Easton Street in July 1939, where she lived with her daughter, Elizabeth: she was still plying the bobbins at 94. She died some time between then and 1945.

caught halfway between Royalist Oxford and Parliamentarian London, it was positively awkward. Different books have described Wycombe as 'an outpost of the Parliamentarian forces' or insisted that 'the townsmen as a body were royalists' who 'fumed and fretted at being unable fully to display their loyalty'. Neither was quite true. Between 1642 and 1644 the town was battled over by the opposing forces, and expressed no obvious opinion of its own. Although it seems that a Puritan group took over the council in the 1650s (when being a Puritan was pretty safe), the main political issue was the management of the charitable sums intended for the poor. One group in the corporation believed that part of the corn toll and the rents from some market stalls should go to support the poor, while another did not and sought to restrict these charitable purposes. The townspeople were concerned enough to riot over the issue in 1649 but, aside from this, played no part in local politics; the arguments took place among a tiny group of about two dozen aldermen and officials. The borough purchased a charter from 'that grand rebell Olliver', as a later Royalist put it, but in 1660 it had it burned and bought a new one. Political

commitment was not a high priority in High Wycombe.

Just as High Wycombe's medieval trades depended on London, so the new industries that arose also produced goods for that ever-growing metropolitan market. Arguably first off the mark was lace-making. The manufacture of pillow lace seems to have come to England late in the 1500s and had certainly reached Wycombe by 1618 when Jane Carter, an orphan, was bound by the Overseers of the Poor as apprentice to John Hawkins to learn the craft; presumably Mrs Hawkins was to teach her, which pushes the arrival of lace-making back another few years. By 1651 the trade was moving into the hands of intermediary lace-buyers such as William Lovell. Sixty years later, the lace-buyers were 'keeping several hundred workmen constantly employed ... These whole-sale men trade weekly to London where they sell their lace'. 'Workmen' was presumably not a gender-specific term, for, while men were the traders in lace, making it was a female business. It was also an indoor one: in 1627 lace-making was referred to as a 'work of house-wifery' and it was commonly resorted to by women to augment the family income. This

23   Rye Mill had gone over from milling corn to making paper by the late 1600s. The Rye Engineering Company used the buildings from the First World War to 1952, and the motor garage which occupies the site today incorporated some fragments of the old structure until very recently.

explains why lace bobbins are found virtually every time the floorboards of an old house in the area are removed or an excavation takes place (in the 1990s they turned up in both Pann Mill and Bassetsbury Manor, for example). But High Wycombe was never the stronghold of lace-making. In 1851 there were 226 lace-makers in the town and its suburbs out of a population of about 4,500; compare this with tiny villages such as Great Kimble with 109 and 204 at Monks Risborough. From the 1860s onwards the old craft, which had become a standby of the very poor, declined under the impact of machine-made lace; and as it was never a pleasant business ('the pallid and sickly appearance of the women and girls who bent day-long over their lace pillows for a pittance was a byword', wrote Ashford) lace-makers were often only too keen to turn to something else. Mrs Bradbury of George Street, for instance, abandoned it on marrying a saw-repairer in 1900, and took up chair-caning instead—a trade which had its own hazards, but was better paid.

The paper industry emerged at roughly the same time and its produce went down the river to the capital as well. The first definite record of paper-making in the Wycombe area comes in 1612 when the will of Edward Isaac mentioned paper-making equipment; he was perhaps working at Glory Mill in Wooburn or Hedge Mill, both first stated to be paper mills in 1627. However, later reports imply that the first Wye valley paper mills were started as early as the 1590s. Whatever the case, the chalk-rich water was ideal for bleaching pulp and the decline of the cloth trade gave paper-making its opportunity: it was easy enough to add a metal bed to a cloth mill and use its hammers to pound rags into paper pulp instead. There were no paper mills in or even near the borough itself (Rye Mill did not go over to paper until the late 1700s), possibly because its restrictions on trade sat uncomfortably with the entrepreneurial paper-masters, and possibly because of active opposition to the ceaseless noise of the

hammers, the risk of disease from rags, the damming of the river and the introduction of 'foreign' workers: all of these were causes of complaint mentioned in a petition to the government in 1636. So it was the down-river hamlets where the industry took hold. In 1798 there were 17 paper workers between the ages of fifteen and sixty in the borough, but 75 in Chepping Wycombe parish outside it, although that had a lower population.

One record gives us a unique glimpse into the 18th-century paper industry. On 15 April 1728 the Mealcock, Ralph Rose's Thames barge, sank near Boulter's Lock on its way down river from Little Marlow, and its load included consignments from several Wye paper-makers who then appealed to the County Court to be refunded the tax on their spoiled paper. The hardest hit, Ralph Spicer of Edge and Glory Mills, had lost paper worth over £53, in the form of '77 bundles of whited brown, 133 reams of ordinary crown, 168 reams of hand crown and 89 reams of blue demi paper'. Other loads included oddities such as 'third pott' and 'grocer's half pound', indicating how specialised paper production already was. John Butcher of Frog Mill, Grace Francis of Loudwater and Jane Bates of Lower Marsh shared in the misfortune, along with paper manufacturers from outside the area.

By 1830 Marsh Mill employed 53 hands, making it the area's biggest employer and outstripping any chair factory. Yet in that very year a disciplined body of paper workers attacked and destroyed the newly-introduced Fourdrinier paper machines at Ash, Marsh, Marsh Green, Loudwater and Snakeley Mills, fearing these contraptions would lose them their jobs. They were right, but only managed to accelerate change by forcing some small paper masters into bankruptcy and leaving the trade in the hands of those who could afford to buy and protect new machinery. By the end of the 19th century, Marsh and Loudwater were dominated by their huge paper enterprises.

24 Edmund Hutchinson, chair-master, who died about 1883. Edmund's son, also Edmund, carved the 'Champion Chair' for the Great Exhibition in 1851, and in the 1870s Hutchinson's furniture was considered to be 'in front of all the rest'. The workshops were originally in St Mary Street, then moved to London Road about 1890. The firm was last recorded in 1907.

It took over a century more for the staple trade of the town to emerge. In 1725 Daniel Defoe referred to the great quantity of Chiltern beech wood 'brought from hence', implying it was not used locally but rather a commodity for export. Daniel Pusey supplied West Wycombe Vestry with Windsor chairs in 1732, but he was the only chair-maker recorded in the area for many years. The first surviving Windsors attributable to a maker come from Slough, not Wycombe, and Wycombe's first attributable piece of furniture is not a chair at all but a cabinet made in the 1790s by James Gomme, whose niece Dinah had taken over

his business by 1830 and who was distantly related to the Gommes of G-Plan fame. The first chair-makers listed in the trade directories were the Treacher brothers, William, Daniel and Samuel, in 1784 and by the 1810s the parish registers were distinguishing between 'chairmakers' and 'chair manufacturers' who owned the factories. Specialisation within the industry was already taking place: in the 1790s William Treacher was making both Windsor and 'fancy' chairs, which would have required a range of different skills, and Charles Skull was described as a 'japanner' of chairs in 1813 (he was a chairmaster ten years later). The development of small factories from the early 1800s allowed this specialisation, and would have an impact on the built environment of the town which long outlasted the heyday of the industry itself. Yet the trade was slow to develop: in 1835 an itinerant Methodist minister found that Downley had a factory employing 'near forty' hands, and even by 1851 the largest factory was Glenister's with 50 hands, followed by Skull's with thirty. These were not colossal businesses. However, between 1841 and 1875 the numbers of people working in chair-making rose about sixfold, and by the latter date James Cox's factory alone employed 150 workers.

The council had less and less to do with these industries, or with the livelihood of the town it was supposed to be governing. Possession of the burgess-ship became important only because it conferred the right to take part in elections for High Wycombe's two MPs. In January 1672, no fewer than 86 new burgesses were elected, half of whom lived outside the Borough, the first 'foreign' burgesses. Some were related to the inhabitants, but all except eight were 'gentlemen' or aristocrats, and it was no coincidence that a Parliamentary by-election was pending at the time. It was certainly no coincidence that the list was headed by Lord Lovelace, who was challenging the local influence of the Earl of Bridgewater, the Lord Lieutenant and Wycombe's High Steward. This marked the start of the local aristocracy coming to see the Borough of Wycombe as an asset to be controlled.

The Earl of Bridgewater was followed in turn by Lord Wharton of Wooburn, the Wallers of Beaconsfield, and the Earl of Shelburne, owner of the Temple Wycombe and Loakes estates. The Waller and Shelburne interests, while politically on different sides, shared the representation of the town for 36 years. Wycombe was not a 'closed' borough, in the sense that it was not actually *owned* by one family, but its limited franchise meant that anyone with enough money could bring 'influence' to bear and ensure their own candidate's election. One instance of this was the building of Wycombe's handsome new Guildhall in 1757, paid for by Shelburne: it was munificence to achieve a political effect. In return, the town exhibited a proudly apolitical attitude little short of cynicism. When the first Lord Wharton, a radical Whig and Dissenter, died in 1715, his friends in the Borough seemed unconcerned that his son and successor was a Jacobite High Tory. In 1790, when Sir John Dashwood-King stood as a vaguely Tory candidate for the 'independence' of the Borough, Wycombe's powers-that-be were so keen to avoid contested elections that an agreement was concluded to share the MPs between the Shelburnes of Loakes and the Dashwoods of West Wycombe. The arrangement held until the Great Reform Act 42 years later.

As the 18th century turned into the 19th, the tiny borough, resolutely turning out to re-elect its unopposed MPs, guarding its rents and revenues, administering its ancient charities, the Grammar School and Hospital, seemed like a cross between Barchester and Trumpton. Despite occasional drives for efficiency—as in 1766 when, in response to dearth and bread riots around the country, it attempted to reinstate the ancient laws of the market—the council was content to allow its powers to pass to other bodies. In 1765 a Court of Quarter Sessions was established, composed of the mayor, recorder,

justice, aldermen and burgesses as well as a jury. Then in 1805 the county magistrates demanded that the Wycombe Court contribute to the county rate. It indignantly refused, but, having done so, had to carry out the county's functions within the borough boundaries, and consequently appointed a borough treasurer and levied a rate. In 1818 it rebuilt the House of Correction. Meanwhile, the council's own revenues came under attack. From 1793 corn dealers began to bring 'sample sacks' of grain to Wycombe market instead of the whole amount to be sold. Eventually the Council's attempt to levy tolls on the sale amount rather than just the samples met resistance, and after 1832 the corn toll produced only about £20 per year. Furthermore, the wealth of High Wycombe increasingly rested on the industries, lace, paper and chairs, that were nothing to do with the antique structures of the borough.

For a while the Paving and Lighting Commission, set up in 1815, became the focus of opposition. At first the mayor chaired its meetings and aldermen sat on it, but by 1821 only one remained. The commission provided ten new street lamps, a night-watchman, and pavements; it compelled the Turnpike Trustees to set gutters along main roads, laid a sewer in Frogmoor in 1825, and began gas lighting in 1832. It was an alternative council and, in fact, much more active than the real one. In 1817, most of the commissioners signed a petition to have the charters published, a move resisted by the mayor and aldermen because they knew the charters did not support their long-exercised right to elect new burgesses. The 'opposition' secured a legal Writ of Quo Warranto against Alderman Thomas Westwood, demanding he prove his right to be a burgess. This case dragged its way through the Court of Chancery until 1830, by which time the agricultural and paper riots were beginning to shade into the general agitation for the passage of the Great Reform Bill. When the bill was eventually passed, it extended the Parliamentary franchise from the borough of Wycombe to the whole parish, and from the burgesses alone to anyone who owned or rented property worth £10, severing forever the intimate link between the borough and its MPs. Three years later the old council was itself swept away by the Municipal Corporations Act, and the new one, elected by all ratepayers, was largely composed of the critics of the old. Even so, Wycombe's characteristic inactivity showed through: the new council decided not to levy a general rate, and even gave up administering the town's charities.

One step towards modernity was the provision of a borough police force. In 1839 the new Watch Committee of the Council appointed the beadle and town crier, George Davis, as 'Superintendent of Police' at £15 per year with a free house next to the churchyard. This office grew out of the responsibilities of the town crier as laid down in 1829, when Thomas Skull was enjoined to 'exert himself to prevent boys and other persons from doing mischief to ... any property belonging to the Corporation'. A year later, Davis was provided with a new Metropolitan Police-type uniform, but it took another ten years before the *ad hoc* assistance he received from night watchmen and parish constables with 'staff, lantern, rattle and belt' was replaced with full-time policemen. Each subsequent change made the force more organised and professional. In 1856 Davis's wage was raised to £90 providing he gave up any other employment, and from 1882 the force qualified on efficiency grounds for government support grants. In 1881 the council voted to keep the Wycombe force separate from the county's, and the town had two police stations, one for each force, right up to 1947. Part of the reason was that a local police force was convenient for some people. At one stage it was alleged that constables went round canvassing for councillors at election time, and one of the main arguments made in favour of independence from the county was that the borough police would not enforce the licensing laws! This sense that the councillors 'owned' the police lessened over time, but one radical commentator recalled that, in the

early 1900s, Lord Carrington's pheasant shoots at Daws Hill resulted in people rushing to the Rye to poach fallen birds, and 'two thirds of Wycombe's small police force were on duty to look after his Lordship's pheasants'!

The police was only the first in a series of modern institutions created through a mixture of voluntary and private effort in these years, as it became clear that the old, haphazard ways of managing were no longer appropriate for an increasingly industrial town. In particular, a town full of chair factories, sawmills and timber yards needed more to fight fires than a pair of stationary water-pumps kept in the church porch, and the arrangements of various fire insurance companies. In 1861, after the failure of a public subscription, the council paid for a new fire engine and an engine house in Frogmoor. By 1868 the climate had changed and a committee of local notables was set up to establish a fire brigade: the first firemen were employed the following year (it is not clear exactly how this differed from what press reports called the 'old brigade' whose 'dis-organisation' was so marked). For many years fire loomed large in the town's life, and for those not directly involved it was almost a social spectacle. 'It was a case of which factory will it be this year?', a local resident recalled as late as 1997. 'The fire engine bells would go at 12 o'clock at night, and you'd rush out to see who it was.' Mrs Denton of Temple Street 'never missed a good fire, even during the war years'. The brigade remained an entirely volunteer service supported by public subscription and attracted some of the most prominent citizens of the town: for instance, architect and five-times Mayor Arthur Vernon was its Captain until 1881.

1875 saw the beginnings of the hospital, another great voluntary effort. This was again an organisation steered by a committee of local dignitaries and, small though its buildings on Priory Road were, its eight beds provided an alternative for the poorer sick to the Wycombe Union's workhouse at Saunderton. In its first year, the Cottage Hospital treated 41 people.

25   Grim-faced Wycombe firemen stand in the wreckage of Castle Brothers chair factory, Desborough Park Road, 27 November 1923. Fire risk in Wycombe made the fire brigade a vitally important institution—though there were plenty of stories of factories burning down just after the insurance policy was renewed!

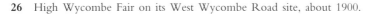

26   High Wycombe Fair on its West Wycombe Road site, about 1900.

Some things remained the same in the Victorian town. Although the corn tolls no longer provided the backbone of the Council's finances, Wycombe's fairs and markets were still great occasions. The *Bucks Free Press*, founded in 1856, was printed on Friday to be ready for the market; and the 1840 diary of Henry Gibbons, a Bledlow Ridge farmer, reveals how important these events were. He had to visit Wycombe most Fridays as a member of the Board of Guardians, but the board's meetings were obviously intended to coincide with market day so that its members would be in town anyway. He regularly used the services of a dealer, Mr Coleman, to sell wheat in the market. The council encouraged the fairs by moving the cattle fair into the High Street in 1838, and began a late-June wool fair at the same time. In 1840 Henry Gibbons found the Easter Monday fair 'tho' tolerably good for sheep, was much injured for cattle' and discovered a local character, Mr Hughe, in whose opinion 'their wise blockheads have spoiled it'. Despite the gripes the fair went on successfully, but times were changing. Gibbons went to Risborough Fair in May and sold a hundred sheep there, while a Mr Adams of Risborough actually called on *him* to buy pigs; he also went to and fro on the new Slough rail line to London to arrange his late uncle James's affairs, though complaining all the while about the cost and the delays he suffered!

People's scope was widening in one sense, and narrowing in another. The Michaelmas fair began to arouse opposition from Wycombe's moralist elements who saw in its entertainments and the thousands of visitors who came for them a threat to the town's character. Some defended the usefulness of the Hiring Fair, and indeed it was important even beyond the agricultural sphere: in 1933 George Cole, still at his bench at Birch's at the age of 96, recalled being hired there as an apprentice chair-maker some eighty years before. The *Free Press*, however, so far as female servants were concerned, 'did not think respectable girls would

now be found standing in the fair for the purpose, nor would respectable employers seek a girl from such a source'. In November 1871, Ashford states, 'the abomination was got rid of' (Wycombe wasn't alone: Chalfont St Peter's fair went in 1872 and in 1879 a meeting demanded the abolition of Marlow Fair). But it was a meagre victory. The stalls and rides were cleared from the High Street, but were simply moved to Peter Greeves's meadow out at Bird-in-Hand, and in 1872 150 youths turned up to be engaged at the Guildhall as usual, attended by a peepshow at The Globe, donkey rides, and 'the fattest woman in the world'! In 1875 the *Free Press* complained that 'interested parties still persist in attempts to perpetuate an abortion of the old fair ... a monstrous nuisance and unmixed evil'. It was still going on in 1908, when the pubs were open from six in the morning to eleven at night, and the Hiring Fair eventually died of its own redundancy, not the efforts of puritans.

Wycombe had grown steadily over the centuries. Probably from the 1200s the huge market place began to be filled in as the shops and stalls maintained by burgesses and traders were converted into permanent buildings, creating Bull Lane, Queen Square, Church Street and so on. The road from the Corn market to Bridge Mill first appeared in the records as 'Bynethebryge' in 1309 and was later known as St Mary Street, while Paul's Row was recorded in 1475. By Tudor times the urbanised area was spilling beyond the borough boundary with buildings such as Temple Farm and what is now Chiltern House further to its east.

The area of meadow west of the town was called Newland before 1227, either because it had been newly drained and made usable then, or because it was newly incorporated within the borough. The council owned cottages in it, and more were built over time. Between 1741 and 1760, for instance, 'several cottages' were built east of the land called the Hop Garden, and other new houses mentioned

27 Tudor Wycombe: the 16th-century fabric of the White House is clearly visible in this photograph taken from its garden in 1924. A number of High Street buildings, like it, hide an older structure behind an 18th-century front-age. The White House (which also houses Elizabethan wall-paintings upstairs) was for many years the home of the Steevens family, prominent local Quakers.

28   Newland Cottage on Desborough Road, the home of the Furness family, painted by Miss M. Furness for one of her brothers. They were the last generation of the family to live in the house. The painting bears the title 'To my darling Reg for his 25th birthday, July 9th '04, in remembrance of his old house'.

in the records probably represent the beginnings of Newland Street. On the south side of Water Lane was Newland Cottage, a large 18th-century house owned by the Furness family who could be classed as gentry. But development began in earnest in the 1820s. John Ivery, an upholsterer, built 11 cottages on the south of Long Row between 1824 and 1828 and at roughly the same time Thomas Miller, a furrier, constructed all the houses on the north side. Miller also had another 14 dwellings built on land opening off Newland Street, which were dubbed Miller's Row. Again, between 1836 and 1838 George Steers, a carpenter, put up 12 cottages on what became known as Newland Meadow. This name recalls how the developers carved up the meadows to form the new streets— meadows whose boundaries could still be

glimpsed on maps years later in the form of streams and walls.

In the 1860s development began again on the north and west half of Newland. The 'Goodearl Deeds' belonging to Wycombe Museum show clearly how Thomas Phillips, a master turner, and the chair manufacturer Edwin Skull bought a plot in what had once been Munday's Mead in 1860, laid out a road along it, and cannily sold it off in bits to various interested parties rather than develop it themselves. Most impressively, they exploited the competition between breweries for the area's new working-class custom by selling a plot to the Wheelers, the Wycombe brewers, which later became the *Rose and Crown*; and another to their Marlow rivals the Wethereds, which was turned into the *Peacock*. They even got the Wethereds to help contribute towards the upkeep of the road—first recorded as 'Mendy Street' in 1862. It was a profitable sideline to making chairs.

On the east side of town there was a parallel if slightly later development prompted by the arrival of the railway. In 1851 there had been only two families resident in 'Town Field', those of William Hutchings, a chair-maker, and Robert Willis, a postman. The railway cut through the existing fields and made it easier to sell them for housing, which south of the line became known as Saffron Platt and north of it, Wheeler's Field (later North Town). The latter name recalled the former hop fields of Wheeler's brewery which had occupied the area. The *Railway Tavern* at the top of Railway Terrace, Railway Place, and names of pubs like the *Steam Engine* and *Porter's Arms* all showed where the area's origins lay. This did not mean that the people living there were all rail workers; in

fact, they were few and far between. In Duke Street in 1875, for instance, only George Smith, a porter, was on the railways; but 17 of his neighbouring 40 householders were, predictably, chair workers.

These eastern developments were more sanitary than Newland, with its open streams and privies emptying into them; and the courts and yards opening off the town centre streets were in a similar condition. These mainly arose from householders of modest means building small houses to the rear of their own. In 1851 Paul's Row, for example, contained Youens Passage, three houses developed by Robert Youens the basket-maker, and next door to it the nine houses of Moody's Yard, built by the maltster James Moody. In 1848 the Mayor, William Rose—one of a dynasty of doctors to have served the town—and the Vicar, Thomas Paddon, managed to get High Wycombe put

29 Edwin Skull's factory, from his broadsheet of 1865. If this picture is accurate (and the landscape is a little romanticised) it is the earliest authentic picture of a Wycombe chair workshop. Skull's went on to become one of the most well-known Wycombe furniture names before being taken over by Ercol in 1934.

30 The Master and pupils of the Old Grammar School, photographed by William Sansome of Easton Street possibly as early as 1860. The school was established after Queen Elizabeth's Charter of 1562 using the revenues of St John's Hospital.

on the itinerary of the inspectors under the Health of Towns Act, much to the annoyance of the council. It 'used every means in its power to prevent the inspection', some positive—setting up a committee to order the cleaning of drains and ditches—and some less so. Through the following summer the inspector was frustrated at every turn. 'In no town have I met such opposition', he declared, but eventually produced a report detailing Wycombe's death rate of more than 23 in every thousand and an accompanying catalogue of sanitary horrors—pigs, people, shared privies, open drains and wells all jammed together in an area Dr Rose referred to as 'the nursery of fever'. The council denied that Wycombe was particularly unhealthy and produced medical witnesses to allege that much of Newland's disease was due instead to its residents' habits. The inspector's report was only advisory; the council was free to ignore it, and did.

But even the council could no longer hold off the advance of modernity. The collapse of the corn toll revenues meant that by 1850 it was £122 in debt, and had no choice but

to levy a rate, which suddenly brought in another £80 per year. There was no great opposition, and this seemed to breach a psychological divide: from then on the council became more activist, more willing to take on responsibility, and more willing to spend money. A new interest in sanitary reform resulted in it establishing a Board of Health in 1865, and it absorbed the functions of its old rival, the Paving and Lighting Commission, the following year.

The council attempted but failed to have its way over one of Wycombe's most antiquated institutions, its run-down three-centuries-old Grammar School on Easton Street, whose Master complained that he risked falling through the floor whenever he crossed the classroom. Its trustees came up with a scheme for renovation in 1873, and the Charity Commissioners drew up plans to expand the school. Wycombe's Reform Association called a meeting in response, chaired by the mayor: they demanded that the new places at the school should be free, and that the funds of the Hospital linked with it should not pay for facilities for middle-class boys, as they had been used for the poor for centuries. If the council had kept control of its charities in 1835 instead of farming them out to trusts, it could have done what it wanted, but the move was not successful. However, more egalitarian educational organisations were starting to flourish: as well as designing the new Grammar School buildings, Arthur Vernon also built Priory Road School—or Cemetery Road, as it was called when first opened in 1875 with room for 1,000 pupils.

In contrast, the council's health campaign met with some success. By 1872 it had driven nearly all domestic pigs from the borough, and in 1874 introduced new by-laws on refuse disposal and the keeping of animals. But any further advance in water supply and drainage came up against the fact that it would require work to be done outside the borough boundary, in the *Parish* of Wycombe; and the parish's governing body, the vestry, was as conservative, jealous of its independence, and resistant to spending money as the council itself had been only a few years before. In 1862 the council tried to brick over the main ditch in Newland, but the far bank lay outside the

31 High Wycombe viewed in 1847 from the vicinity of Keep Hill, from an engraving by E.J. Neimann. A somewhat romanticised view, but one which gives a clear idea of the relationship of the town to the landscape as it remained substantially until the 1930s.

borough and the vestry would not co-operate. Ten years later a joint drainage scheme was explored but foundered; then in 1873 the council, prompted by the unwelcome prospect of a private waterworks in Wycombe, proposed that it should set up its own, buy the existing private gasworks, and extend its boundaries to include the whole of the parish, uniting the entire area under one authority for drainage, water supply, education, police and fire-fighting. It was an ambitious plan indeed—too ambitious for the vestry, and even for the townspeople, who voted it down at a heated public meeting.

But the end-game approached. The 1875 Public Health Act ordered local sanitary authorities to devise comprehensive drainage schemes and, although the vestry still demurred, a *coup de grace* was issued by the Thames Conservancy Board in 1879. It announced it would no longer tolerate the pollution pouring down the Wye from Wycombe's factories and mills. In response, the council declared it would set up a sewage works for the borough alone. The parish contained as much industry as the borough, but the vestry was in no position to take similar measures on its own. It had no choice but to concede. In June 1880, the Chepping Wycombe Extension Act became law, pushing the borough boundary out eastwards into the parish to include Wycombe Marsh, north to North Town and Hughenden Road, and west as far as Bird-in-Hand. For the first time Chepping Wycombe borough had grown to match the physical growth of the town; and the extension was a belated recognition that the world had moved on from the days when High Wycombe was governed by the ringing of the market bell.

Three

Furniture Town
(1880–1932)

It would be an exaggeration to state that the borough extension opened the floodgates to new development, but it did seem to facilitate it. There were already new streets to the west (Brook, Regent and Westbourne Streets), and an isolated three in Oak Mead (Desborough, Victoria and Shaftesbury Streets). Within ten years the area as far as Desborough Avenue was full of houses (few survive, but the terraces of West End Road are still dated between 1883 and 1891), and another ten took development west to Oakridge Road. In this situation, Wycombe's great social institutions saw clearly where their duty lay. A new 'iron church' of St John was built in Desborough Road in 1882, and in 1895 the *Saracen's Head* moved from its old site in Frogmoor to a lavish pseudo-Indian building in Green Street to serve the area's new working-class customers. A second boundary extension in 1901 brought Fryers Lane, Terriers, and the margins of Loudwater within the borough.

Arthur Bradbury was born in one of these new houses, 13 George Street, in 1904:

The house was situated on the end of a row of cottages, and had two rooms down and two bedrooms. There was a stretch of about four yards of cobblestones, and then a woodhouse, not very large, but [which] contained a sink, a built-in copper, a splash-down toilet and room for coal and firewood. The water had to be drawn from a hand-pump ... It was a dreary place, and when I look back over the years, I fully realise that word 'slum', for that's all I can think it was.

Two adults and four children shared this little house. Until such dwellings began to be extended later on, this was the pattern for hundreds of families.

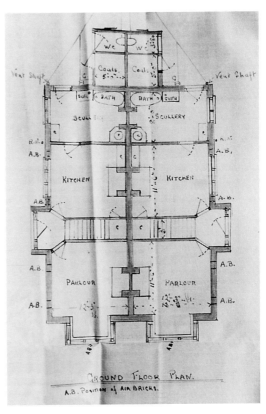

GROUND FLOOR PLAN.
A.B. Position of AIR BRICKS.

32 Plan of a pair of three-bedroom, semi-detached houses to be built on land owned by Ford's papermills in Station Road, Loudwater, in 1925. Such houses were typical of the hundreds built in Wycombe in the 1920s and 1930s: a far cry from the Victorian terraces.

33 Aged 96 when she was photographed by Henry Blackwell for the *Daily Sketch* in 1930, this lady was supposedly Wycombe's oldest chair-caner. We believe her name was Hester Milner.

And these families, housed in the new terraces, were overwhelmingly those of chair workers. In the 1891 Census, Baker Street contained 37 households, headed by 35 people in employment of some sort. Of these, 23 were working in the furniture industry (if we include William Boot, the sawmill labourer); and two of the others, the carmen Thomas Batchelor and Jacob Hill, were probably carters for the chair factories. Even counting all the people whose occupation was listed, we find 57 out of 88 were chair workers, from caning girls like Sarah and Fanny Chilton to Thomas Nash, a chair-master who resided at the end of the street in 'Faith Villa'.

Sheahan's estimate of the town's output in 1862 had been 'a chair a minute'; in 1875 it was '4,700 per day' and by 1884 the single order of 19,300 chairs for an evangelical meeting in London had worked its way into local folk-lore. Furthermore, Wycombe was beginning to think of chair-making as its symbol. In 1876 the council presented a chair to the mayor of Calais, the first recorded instance in an endless series of such gifts to dignitaries and celebrities. Two chairs went to Queen Victoria on the occasion of her 1887 Jubilee, a child's chair 'from the children of High Wycombe' and one carved in 17th-century oak from the belfry of Hughenden Church. When the Queen actually visited the town in 1877 as a guest of Disraeli at Hughenden Manor, the council decided to mark the occasion by deputing Councillor Walter Skull to organise his fellow chair-masters and erect an arch of chairs over the High Street beside the Guildhall, beneath which the Queen would pass. It was clear from this one gesture that *Wycombe* and *chairs* were becoming synonymous.

As well as dominating the town economically, the furniture trade had an increasing effect on it physically. It took very little capital to start a chair-making business and some of the very largest firms began from a shed workshop in a back garden: Ebenezer Gomme, for instance, started in 1895 the enterprise which was to become G-Plan in one of these back-yard workshops behind his house in Totteridge Road. This meant parts of the town became overrun with tiny furniture businesses, crammed in beside houses and to the rear of pubs. At the other end of the scale, the largest companies were altering the whole environment around them. In 1881 the Goodearl family bought Moses Gibson's chair workshop in Mendy Street to add to their factory in West End Road. Two years later John Crook, another chair-master, bought 21-31 Long Row, pulled some of the cottages down and used others for work-shops and stores; together with the *Peacock Inn* and two more cottages, the Goodearls bought

34 Plumridge's sawmills, Desborough Road, about 1900. Naturally sawmills were an important component of the Furniture Town. Beginning on a site in Denmark Street before 1875, Jonathan Plumridge added a second at Desborough Road by 1895. After the Second World War the business concentrated in Bridge Street, where it still survives.

35 J. Mole's furniture factory at Springfield in 1919, a typical medium-sized chair works. Mole's made invalid furniture between about 1907 and 1935.

36 A symbolic moment for the Furniture Town: the chair arch erected to commemorate Queen Victoria's visit to Wycombe in 1877.

them in 1890 to be used as engine rooms, making shops and a travelling crane shelter. At intervals through the 1890s they purchased another 12 cottages in Newland Meadow, and turned them into sheds and workshops as well. Thus the older areas of the town gradually shifted in character from residential to industrial use.

At first, most chair-masters kept apart from the government of the town and it held aloof from them. Two factors combined to change this. During a debate in the House of Commons in the 1870s—the exact date seems to be unrecorded—Randolph Churchill referred sneeringly to Wycombe's output of 'cheap and nasty' furniture. Their pride stung, manufacturers such as Skull, Hutchinson, Caffall & Keen and Nicholls & Janes tried to raise quality in the industry. Sometimes this meant making reproductions of antique chairs; on several occasions, Ralph Janes was asked by antique dealers to make up complete sets from 'original' pieces which turned out to be his own handiwork! Birch's, in particular, shook off the traditional conservatism of the Wycombe furniture trade and employed rising designers such as E.G. Punnett to design pieces strongly influenced by the Arts and Crafts movement, and sold them to Liberty's and other stores. Much of this change involved bringing in outside talent. Birch's raised the standard of its upholstery work after a strike by its London workforce shifted the balance in the upholstery section to Wycombe, where the number of upholsterers tripled. About 1887, Bridon's set up a 'best chairmaking department' in Queen's Road, importing a Mr Manders from Norwich and a Mr Rudd from Barnstaple to work there. The

firm eventually moved to Shoreditch to be close to the technical institutes, where several Wycombe craftsmen went to study carving, in particular. In these ways, the chair trade gathered respect as well as economic power.

Secondly, the masters were encouraged into a more activist attitude by their men. Sporadic attempts to form trade unions were matched by efforts to form employers' organisations, and on occasions the two worked in tandem. In 1872 the council chamber was used for the union's first recruitment meeting, while the attempts to re-establish it in 1891 were greeted warmly by some employers. In 1907 the War Office rejected the Wycombe firms' tenders for barrack furniture after noticing that the prices were all the same; Alderman Birch admitted that there was a 'ring', but argued this was necessary to prevent undercutting and sweated labour. In hard times, chair-masters could even be found running soup kitchens for their former employees.

37 Payne's Yard to the rear of the *Antelope* in Church Square. It was called Dancer's Yard before William Payne took over William Dancer's carting business here in the 1840s. The Paynes left between 1907 and 1911. From a drawing by Francis Colmer, 1944.

38   Birch's, Denmark Street. This state-of-the-art factory, built in 1896, represented a move away from the old-fashioned wooden workshops towards production on a grander scale.

39   Despite appearances, 84-year-old George Cole is not the guest of honour at this 1921 party at Birch's factory. Instead it seems to have been a wedding party for Miss E.K. Walters, soon to become Mrs Coombs. But which lady was she?

40   The paper-workers' union float, ready for a procession about 1910.

Not all employers were so magnanimous: not all could afford to be. The conditions described by the *Bucks Free Press* in 1857 were true for years afterwards:

> Evidence of the superficial prosperity of this neighbourhood is to be found in the numbers of little master men who spring up in a day, and as rapidly disappear, which keeps the whole trade in a fretful state of competition. Men with hardly sufficient capital to start a load of chairs commence their business by hawking their goods at the nearest available point, underselling the resident tradesmen, ... and at the same time damaging the character of the home manufacturer by the sale of badly constructed goods.

Such masters, if they survived, could scarcely avoid being hard-nosed, hard-hearted, and sometimes plain hard. Stories of the 'tommy-shop' and the 'Custom of the Trade'—men renting their own bench space, or paying for their lamp oil—are still notorious, and the penny-pinching habits of some masters were long dying. Henry Broom, founder of engineers Broom & Wade, gave up making furniture machinery in disgust in 1910 after Thomas Glenister, who had already argued a five per cent discount out of him, turned up to collect his order and demanded another five per cent off for cash. 'He insisted, so I burned all the drawings and patterns and went all out for air compressors.' At another firm in the 1930s, the manager was the boss's son and would time the jig-operators while they made a new pattern. 'As he was a practical man we couldn't pull a fast one,' recalled one employee. '"There", he'd say, "That took so long and when you do more, you will get quicker" and so knocked

41 Thomas Glenister, High Wycombe's first chair-master to be mayor, in 1889.

This new governing class was only one generation away from the cottages, and it was understandable if its representatives were a little rough and ready. The *Free Press* reported that 1894's new mayor, Richard Goodearl, 'started out very low down on the social ladder. It is his boast that he commenced work at 18 pence a week', and he was 'at work long before boys nowadays leave school, and, as a consequence, the education he received was somewhat scanty'. The chair-masters were also a close-knit society, as far as competition would allow. Benjamin Cartwright's grandson Charley, for instance, married one of Benjamin Goodearl's daughters, while his daughter Edith married Owen Haines, founder of yet another firm. Owen's son William in turn married Ethel, one of the nine daughters of Boaz Wooster whose small factory was in Railway Place.

For a long while these new masters of the town had to co-exist with the old, most prominent among whom were the Wheeler family. Robert Wheeler came to Wycombe from London in 1808 to go into partnership with the brewer Andrew Biddle, and quickly became the most prominent brewer in the area. He was already mayor by 1812, and served as the last mayor of the old corporation in 1834. Robert, his sons and grandsons together held the mayoralty 21 times between them. Francis Wheeler was borough treasurer in 1887, and his cousin Henry took over after his death until the First World War. Many Wheelers were borough or county magistrates as well as being involved in the community in all sorts of ways. The Henry Wheelers, uncle and nephew, were masters of Wycombe Marsh Paper Mill, and Thomas, as well as being Treasurer of the Rural Sanitary Authority and the Poor Law Union, was still helping at the Christ Church Sunday School at the age of 84 (Christ Church, a low-church breakaway from All Saints, was mocked in its early years as 'the Wheelers' Church'). Henry junior was captain of the fire brigade in 1891; Robert Drew Wheeler served as captain of Wycombe's company of Rifle

off so many minutes.' At least one boss was paying his workers in cash out of his back pocket into the 1960s.

Still, in 1889 Thomas Glenister was elected mayor of High Wycombe, the first chair manufacturer to hold the office, and was re-elected the following year. He was followed by Richard Goodearl in 1894, and Walter Birch was mayor four times between 1900 and 1916. For two periods—1911 to 1924 and 1929 to 1934—each and every mayor was a chair-master, and by the end of 1935 all the borough's distinguished aldermen—Messrs Butler, Ellis, Graefe, Haines, Lord, Tilling and Tyzack—were either furniture makers or suppliers of materials to the factories. There could be no clearer sign of High Wycombe's economic and social dominance by this one industry.

42 A candidly informal group of town dignitaries in about 1930. Left to right: Harry Aldridge, the grocer; George Miles, fire chief; Jack Gibson and Jack Williams, chair manufacturers; Mr King; Hubert Glenister; Aleck Stacey; Ralph Janes; and Richard Graefe, the marquetry manufacturer.

43 George Wheeler, grandson of Robert Wheeler senior (founder of the brewery) and mayor of High Wycombe in 1876, 1885 and 1886.

44 Laying the foundation stone of the sewage works east of Funges Farm in 1882. In the centre of the party is the mayor, Thomas Wheeler.

Volunteers; and Dr Humphrey Wheeler of Dial House amassed an impressive list of medical appointments with local bodies. 'The name Wheeler must almost have been synonymous with Wycombe politics' says one writer, and in 1874, during a particularly fractious election campaign, Lord Carrington's nephew R.H. Crewe reportedly fumed 'the political influence of *that family* can be and shall be put down and stamped out. I shall not be satisfied until every member of it is removed from the Town Council'.

Although the brewery was the source of Wheeler power (in 1849 they owned 20 of Wycombe's 42 pubs, including all the ones in

and leading off the High Street apart from Wellers' *Crown* and the *Red Lion*), their control really came as much from the Wycombe Bank. This had been established by Robert Wheeler before 1830 as a branch of the Reading Bank, and by 1888 had offices in Beaconsfield, Risborough and Amersham before being absorbed by the Capital and County Bank in 1896. The bank stood close to the brewery in Easton Street, surrounded by the houses of the Wheelers themselves. 'It was a common sight to see the smaller chair bosses queuing outside the bank on Saturday mornings ... to borrow money to pay their workers.' There was no doubt who was in charge.

In late Victorian and Edwardian Wycombe George Wheeler was said to be only one of the 'Big Three who ... sought to guide the destinies of the old town on progressive lines'; and the others also represented parts of Wycombe's power structure. Arthur Vernon was an auctioneer's son who became an architect and was responsible for much of the town's built environment, while Daniel Clarke, last of the 'Big Three', was town clerk for decades and also served on numerous committees and boards. He bought Castle Hill, north of the town centre, from his in-laws the Peaces, and the two families in turn connected with other prominent lineages in Wycombe. A good illustration of how this close-knit society worked was another figure who was outside the 'Big Three' but who was as active as any of them. Charles W. Raffety, auctioneer and land dealer, was a

trustee of the hospital (along with alderman Haines and Daniel Clarke's son Arthur) and collected the funds for its construction. He was a director of the local Building Society, the Savings Bank and the Water Company, and was for 30 years chairman of the High Wycombe Timber Company. He was a founder member of the fire brigade and started the Chamber of Commerce. When the library was on the brink of foundering, and its benefactor, James Olliff Griffits, ran out of funds, Mr Raffety collected the subscriptions which saved it. Both Arthur Vernon and Charles Raffety died in 1926; Henry S. Wheeler lived on until 1934, but by that time the brewery had been closed for five years and the Wheelers had long ceased to play any part in running High Wycombe. 'England's Furniture Town' was now simply too large and too complex for its

45 Easton Street and the High Street looking westwards in about 1900. The vehicle which has halted outside Dial House on the Crendon Street corner is probably a municipal water cart for sluicing down the roads.

46 An advert from just before the First World War. Richard Davenport Vernon was a cousin of Arthur Vernon, the architect, and carried on his father's business in building materials before setting up an ironmongery in 1872. Motor repairs and sales gradually took over.

47 The derelict brewery buildings on Easton Street, just before their demolition in 1930.

'destinies' to be 'guided' by a little group of well-to-do-families.

The influence of the Abbey on the town was also lessening. Robert Smith, later Lord Carrington, purchased the Loakes estate from Lord Shelburne in 1798 and over the next few years employed James Wyatt to remodel the house as Wycombe Abbey, a grey, castellated Gothic fantasy. His son entered the political fray in the 1830s in the Conservative interest and, although the family soon became staunch

Liberals, they were forever at odds with the borough politicians who nominally shared the same party label. In 1896 the Carringtons had just purchased Gwydor Castle in Wales and determined to dispose of the Abbey. Daws Hill remained within the family, but the sale of 17 farms from Oakridge to Loudwater and south to Well End, along with the Abbey and its 326-acre park, signalled a huge change. The Abbey was bought for £20,000 by the Girls' Education Company under the energetic leader-

48 Noel Leigh's timber yards at Dashwood Avenue operated from the mid-1920s to 1965. This photograph was taken in 1928.

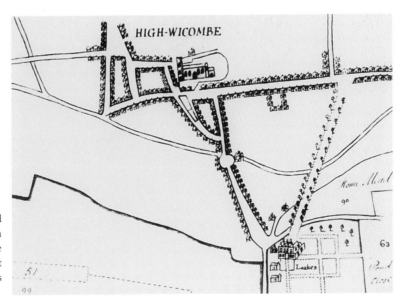

49 The oldest authenticated map of High Wycombe, from a Loakes estate plan of 1763. The buildings are only schematic but the general pattern of streets seems fairly accurate.

50 This detail taken from a print of 1787 entitled 'Wycombe House' is the only surviving picture of the former condition of Loakes Manor before its Gothicisation by Lord Carrington in the early 1800s.

51 The Bucks Militia parading at Wycombe Abbey in 1854, as depicted by the *Illustrated London News*. The training was possibly in preparation for the Militia's participation in the Crimea campaign.

52 McIlroys on the corner of Priory Road and Church Street, the first of High Wycombe's great shopping emporia.

ship of Frances Dove, former mistress at St Leonard's School in St Andrews. In 1929 the Abbey School finally purchased Daws Hill together with a further 200 acres of land.

Despite its changing character, Wycombe was still a centre for the surrounding area, and in fact this centrality was adopting more modern forms. Firstly, the High Street market was becoming a source of cheap goods rather than agricultural produce, especially after the dealers William & Brown removed the cattle market (which had amounted to little for years) from the ring beside the Guildhall to Frogmoor in 1907. The last hour of the Saturday market was a useful opportunity for the poor to buy at a discount as prices were knocked down to make sales. Alison Uttley found this was still the case in 1950, when the market boasted 'cabbages and apples, plums and damsons, pots

and pans, flowers and plants ... heaped on the wooden stalls'. Then, in 1899, the forerunner of modern department stores opened on Church Street in the shape of McIlroy's, a branch of a Reading firm. This was the only emporium of its kind in the district, and attracted people from far and wide. 'The shop made you feel in wonderland. All the staff were in black and white. When you made a purchase, your money was put into little tubes: they pulled a wire and the tube shot off all round the shop on overhead rails to the cash desks, then came back with the change.' By the 1930s, the arrival of McIlroy's Father Christmas in the town on the last Saturday in November was a great occasion. His procession was headed by the Town Military Band, and went via a figure-of-eight route to the store, travelling as far as Desborough Avenue and Gordon Road.

53 Arthur Bailey and his father Joseph outside their clothing store at 130 Desborough Road, about 1900.

High Wycombe exerted a pull on its satellite villages in other ways. Naphill villagers would come walking through Downley on their way to work in the town in the mornings, and in the 1930s new pupils at the Grammar School came from the villages to be 'kitted out' at Hull, Loosley & Pearce in Oxford Street. Bus services made travel easier, and bound the peripheral areas into the centre. In 1892 Lewellyn Weston, a coach builder of Castle Street, started a horse bus service which ran to West Wycombe and Loudwater from the lamp-post opposite Corporation Street. A motor-bus service from Thame in 1907 proved abortive, and it was not until 1912 that Weston's 'Livery Posting Company' went over to motor buses; Frederick Sugg's Penn Bus Company started a motor service in 1920 and, by 1926, Downley (for example) had a bus link direct to the town centre. But the villages—and even portions of the town—still had an independent identity. Wycombe Marsh in the 1930s had two butchers, two bakers, a milkman, and six or seven pubs: apart from shopping for clothes, or to visit the market, there was little need to leave the village. Rose Smith recalled that, growing up in the Desborough area, 'we didn't hardly go into the town at all', although her family did go to London to see plays and go shopping.

The growing town was increasingly a socially divided one as well. The middle-class 'flight to the suburbs' had begun by the early 1870s, when Arthur Vernon the architect and John Parker the solicitor moved off the High Street to new mansions on Amersham Hill. The Furnesses of Newland Cottage had seen their surroundings change from a leafy lane to a working-class slum with a gasworks next door to boot, and by 1899 they had moved to Wycombe Marsh. William Loosley, founder of builders, cabinet makers, outfitters and funeral directors Hull, Loosley & Pearce, left the house over the 'works' to move to Riversleigh on the London Road about 1890. Walter Birch provided the most spectacular instance in the form of The Grange, a great turreted redbrick house on Amersham Hill built in 1899. The new, fragrant villas along the main roads were even attracting outsiders, 'who can combine business in London with residence in a real country town', as a guide book put it. Yet Wycombe's 'great house' period lasted forty years at the most: by 1933 The Grange was a nursing home, and the Wheelers' house on Easton Street, The Limes, was housing the Conservative Club.

Part of the reason for this change was the collapse in the number of girls, in particular, 'going into service' in the 1920s. Until after the First World War, 'nearly all the girls went into service. You had to because there was nothing else to do' unless you had a trade like chair caning. 'Going into service' occurs in narrative after narrative from this time. The girls' experience varied widely. Margaret Dobson, under-parlourmaid at Terriers House, found that Dr and Mrs Priestley treated the servants as 'part of the furniture'; but Gertrude Pitt, a publican's daughter in service to the Hulls at Brigg House on Amersham Hill, was known as 'Pitsey' and treated as one of the family. 'The servants were expected to consume everything the family left, and the provisions were so generous that Pitsey reckoned she could barely squeeze out of the back door by the time she left.' But there was already no butler at Terriers House—the maids did the 'butling'— and the Clarkes at Castle Hill had only a domestic (who didn't even live in the house despite its having room for a whole set of servants), and a gardener in a cottage in the grounds. Grandiose household establishments were less and less possible to maintain.

If there was an institution which united the classes, it was the church—or, to be more accurate, the chapel, for the Anglican church had a far lower profile than its many Nonconformist counterparts which seemed to stand on every street. Sometimes the dividing line wasn't clear: the dominance of the chapels was such that Mr Raffety, an ardent free churchman,

54 An advert for Rupert Mealing's tobacconist's and hairdresser's, from a pre-First World War map of High Wycombe. The Mealings were a well-known and prolific Wycombe family which included several chair manufacturers.

could complacently feel that the Anglican parish church 'belonged' to him and his fellow Dissenters, and even chapel-going families wanted their children christened in the C. of E. People would save them up to be 'done' at one go: and some ended up going through the ritual twice at different churches 'to make sure'! On 23 July 1908, Frederick Bravington, a chairmaker of 38 Oakridge Road, and his wife Emily brought no fewer than nine children to St John's for baptism, aged from a month to eleven.

Olive Pearce recalled how 'Oxford Road chapel became the centre of our social life, as most chapels were', and in Marsh in the '20s and '30s 'life revolved around the pubs if you were a drinker, or the churches if you weren't'. What children remembered most clearly was the Sunday School Treat, as it was the closest many of them got to a holiday, and at the very least injected colour and fun into a relatively grey environment. Union Chapel's Treat in the 1890s was only a trip to a meadow by the Wye a quarter of a mile away, 'but they marched there in style' behind banners and a band; later, more adventurous groups went out to Burnham Beeches, which 'was regarded as foreign parts because it seemed to be a tremendous journey'. In any case, the Sunday School Treat was 'the most exciting day of the year'.

The chapels were in the supporting hands of the chair-masters, which gave them a political as well as a social importance. 'I like these Methodists with their long solemn faces and deep breeches pockets', R.H. Crewe enthused when reviewing the Abbey influence in the 1874 council elections: 'They are our best friends in the Borough'. Henry Goodearl, the ex-mayor's brother, laid the foundation stone for the Terriers Methodist Chapel in 1900, and when Alderman Henry Tilling died in 1939 the *Free Press* stated 'it would be difficult to enumerate the offices which he held', not just at his own Wycombe Marsh Methodist Church, but at those in Penn, Beaconsfield, and Oxford Road. 'He was one of the pillars of the Free Methodist cause—and

every honour that denomination could give, he had well earned.' Frederic Hull of Hull, Loosley & Pearce helped to build the Union Chapel's Memorial Hall with his own middle-class hands: 'Frederic cheerfully spent every moment of his spare time on the work ... going straight from a long day at the business to work for hours as a bricklayer's labourer.'

This did not mean that High Wycombe was a community without conflict. In fact, the ten years before the First World War were, arguably, the most violent and lawless in its history, and some of the agitations could be traced directly to its nature as a chapel-going, Liberal town. In 1904 Parliament passed an Education Act which provided for Church of England schools to be funded from the public rate—a measure unpopular with Nonconformists, who began a non-payment campaign. Wycombe's first sale of the property of such 'passive resisters' took place outside the police station in April 1905. Councillors and chapel ministers attended, and all was peaceful until one man started bidding in earnest for the lots and had to be taken into the station for his own safety. At a trial of passive resisters in 1908, one magistrate left the bench to join the defendants. 1911 was marked by protests about the closure of footpaths. On 5 March four hundred people cut fences and uprooted posts at Desborough Castle while a choir sang the stirring words from the Liberal marching song, 'God gave the land to the people!'. A week later 4,000 people attended the mass-trespass, which soon spread to farmland elsewhere.

By December 1909, regular attacks on evangelist Charles Hatton's mission meetings had grown so severe (mobs of 3,000 were turning up to cause trouble) that the police refused to guarantee him protection. On 6 December Miss Despard, a Suffragette, was shouted down at an Independent Labour Party meeting in the Guildhall and sulphuretted hydrogen was let off, while 10,000 townspeople turned out to pelt the Suffragette marchers on their way from Carlisle to London—though,

55 The old Quaker Meeting House, Crendon Street, drawn by Francis Colmer in 1929.

56 Sunday School Treat: photographed about 1900, this Wesleyan Methodist procession gives an idea of the importance of the chapels in Wycombe people's lives.

to be fair, they already 'bore marks of ill-treatment at Thame and Wheatley', and would receive more at Beaconsfield and Gerrards Cross, while on other occasions the movement in Wycombe was left unmolested. In 1913, a bitter and occasionally violent three-month strike, the first in forty years, paralysed the furniture factories.

But the most shocking of these events was the 1910 election riot. Liberal Wycombe was now surrounded, and, in electoral terms, swamped by a Conservative rural hinterland, and Sir Alfred Cripps's victory in that year did not go down well with many townspeople. The Tories had filled a 'Dump Shop' with imported goods which they claimed would flood the country under the Liberals' 'free trade' policies, and on the announcement of the result this, along with Cripps's committee rooms and the Conservative Club, was attacked. As the Dump Shop blazed, the crowd slashed the fire brigade's hoses. Eighty constables arrived from the county to help the borough's tiny force. On the Saturday night after the poll between six and seven thousand people gathered in the High Street, facing a cordoned-off Guildhall. Finally—at the insistence of the Borough Chief Constable Oscar Sparling, some said, or the County's Deputy Chief Constable—the Mayor read the Riot Act by the light of a bicycle lamp: Philip Stratton, a clerk at Vernon's architects who was given time off to work for the Cripps campaign, 'saw a woman walk up and spit in his face'. Ten minutes later the police and mounted yeomanry charged the crowd, 'paying off some old scores for what they had had to endure all the evening'. Thirty to forty people needed medical treatment and some were left in the street 'bleeding and unconscious'. Lawrence Chadwick, the Sanitary Inspector, and his wife came upon the riot after playing cards with the matron at Booker Hospital, and 'had never run so quick either before or since'.

Riots notwithstanding, High Wycombe in the first third of the 20th century was a self-confident, proudly independent community. Even those conflicts themselves bore witness to a contest to control the body politic, not a feeling that the body politic was irrelevant or not worth fighting over. Furthermore, the town's thriving industry and services drew in more and more people and required more organising. After 1901, there were further boundary extensions in 1927, adding Sands, Castlefield, Cressex, the Abbey Park, and Micklefield, and again in 1934 with the incorporation of West Wycombe and Booker; but these alone could not explain the rise in population, from about 13,000 in 1881 (the borough and parish combined) to about 29,000 in 1928.

The First World War, in particular, brought thousands of people into the town. At one time the astonishing number of 27,000 soldiers needed accommodating: 'the place was stuffed with troops' with the Rifle Brigade quartered broadly at the west end of the town, the Royal Field Artillery in the centre, and the Durham Light Infantry on the east. Churches and the Guildhall were used as messes. The munitions factories also attracted new (and largely female) arrivals—a thousand of these women were left unemployed by 1919.

Speedier communications made it easier for people to come to Wycombe. The town had been a rail terminus since 1854; in 1862 the line was put through to Bicester and Birmingham, but travellers to and from London still had to change trains at Maidenhead. The Great Western and Central Railway companies began planning a joint line linking directly with Marylebone, buying up land to the rear of Gordon Road for the purpose in the early 1900s. The required engineering works claimed lives just as the original construction of the line had done: six men died in the collapse of a new tunnel at Holtspur in 1902, to be commemorated by a monument in Wycombe Cemetery. The new line opened in April 1906, and hundreds of children were given the day off school to ride on special trains; 250 children came from Haddenham alone.

57 Building the Gordon Road rail arch in 1904–5, in preparation for the new line.

58   The town from the Bellfield, about 1880. This view differs from earlier, similar ones in showing the houses along Priory Road to the left of the railway line along the hillside. It also makes very clear the impact of the railway on the town, slicing through the north side of the valley.

In the 1840s people believed the railway, with the nearest station miles away close to Maidenhead, had devastated the town's trade from road traffic, but this turned out to be a temporary effect—if it was ever anything more than exaggeration. Certainly the surviving coaching inns flourished; the *Red Lion*, in particular, became a focal point of the town, and its function rooms the venue for any event which was not actually municipal business, such as the first annual dinner of the Wycombe Chair Manufacturers' Association in 1890, or six years later the auction of the Carrington estates. In 1894 it was said that 'it seems next to impossible to separate the *Red Lion* from High Wycombe, or High Wycombe from the *Red Lion*', and the old inn boasted stabling for 45 horses as well as the town's only coffee rooms.

Wycombe was acquiring other symbols of its identity. High Wycombe Football Club was formed in October 1871 (a season later than Marlow FC), but was destined to be over-taken by a far less formal club which grew out of the Saffron Platt pubs to enable local lads to play matches against village teams. This outfit was playing matches as early as 1884, but only got its name of 'Wycombe Wanderers' after a meeting at the *Steam Engine* pub three years later. The club moved to Loakes Park in 1895, where it was to stay for 95 years, the enduring focus of local enthusiasm and support—so much so, indeed, that when the Wanderers played Bishop Auckland for the Amateur Cup at Wembley in 1957, even Amersham Town FC chose to ignore their scheduled Spartan League match and went to watch Wycombe. The Wanderers, in appreciation, paid their fine.

59   The dapper Mr Lee, licensee of the *Falcon Hotel* in the 1920s.

60   The dance floor of the *Red Lion*, *c*.1934. The *Red Lion*, one of the most venerable of Wycombe's coaching inns, traced its history back to the 15th century. In the 1820s it upgraded itself to a 'hotel' and became a great centre of town life. However it struggled after the Second World War and closed, to considerable local sadness, in 1969.

61   Wycombe Wanderers, about 1990, at their new ground, Adams Park, after the move from Loakes. Verco, the Chapel Lane office furniture manufacturers, sponsored the club between 1988 and 2002.

This age of growth and change also revived—or perhaps invented—antique rituals to express the town's identity. The ex-Town Clerk, John Parker, alluded in his history of Wycombe in 1878 to the annual custom of weighing the mayor, and claimed it had fallen into disuse after the dissolution of the old Corporation in 1835—though it was very curious that no earlier antiquarian had mentioned so singular a ceremony. Whatever the truth, in 1892 the mayor-elect, Charles Harman Hunt, suggested 'reviving' it, and with breaks it has continued ever since. In 1911 the council decided to begin 'Beating the Bounds' of the borough again, a ceremony which had last been held in 1880 (and before that there had been a gap since 1846). The perambulation out as far as Terriers and Loudwater already

took a full day, and after the later boundary extensions it became completely unfeasible. It was not until the 1980s that the event was revived yet again using a modified version of the medieval boundaries.

There were more tangible signs of corporate identity too. In 1901 the council constructed a thoroughfare linking the High Street with Castle Street; it was supposed to be the new home for the Post Office and the council offices, hence its eventual name of Corporation Street, but the Post Office remained obstinately in Easton Street and in the event the administrative centre of the town was moved elsewhere. Now that Wycombe Abbey was sold, Lord Carrington's carriage drive leading from the High Street through the castellated Rupert Gates served no purpose, and

62 Preparing to weigh the mayor at the Guildhall, probably in the 1940s. The weighing apparatus is that still used in the ceremony today.

63 Well-prepared with boots and sticks, the official party gets ready to set off from the *Nag's Head* on London Road to 'Beat the Bounds' on 8 November 1911.

64 A beadle of the borough before the First World War. This photograph has always been said to show one 'Noah Pierce', but the offices of beadle, town crier or mace bearer were held by members of the Davis family for well over 100 years until the 1920s.

in 1901 he remodelled it as Queen Victoria Road; in 1902 this new thoroughfare was offered to the council along with a plot for the long-planned Town Hall, which was finally opened in 1904. It was not until the 1930s that the intended suite of public buildings did finally emerge, but, as with so much at the time, the florid Italianate architecture of the Town Hall marked a decisive breach with the past.

One after another, the council took control of the institutions needed to improve the town, but it was not an easy process. At the time of the Borough Extension in 1880, apart from the police constables, there was only one full-time council official, the Borough Surveyor, who was 'the kingpin on whom all the public works of the town hinged'. The most urgent task was the creation of an efficient drainage, sewerage and water supply system. The first two of these were achieved by 1882, notwithstanding the bankruptcy of the contractors. As for the water supply, it was not until 1900 that the Water Company, whose pumphouse was on Easton Street and whose presence had aroused such opposition in the 1870s, was finally absorbed within the public services, and the Borough Surveyor added the title of Water Works Manager to his list of responsibilities. Eventually the Surveyor's burdens were eased by the employment of a Sanitary Inspector. Lawrence Chadwick, the first, who was to hold the post for 40 years, arrived in 1904, and when the new Public Health Department was created two years afterwards, he kitted out its office at 25 Easton Street with second-hand furniture and converted the pantry into a lab for testing water samples. It was years before he was allowed an assistant; and until 1919 the Health Visitor came for half a day each week from Slough, a town half High Wycombe's size. There had been refuse collections since the 1860s, but more and more regulation of the matter appeared in later municipal by-laws and in 1910 Councillor Aleck Stacey was awarded a contract to collect all the borough's rubbish. The council also made use of water carts to spray the streets in summer.

The council began regulating even the private affairs of its citizens for the public good in a way it would not have dared at one time, making full use of the scope allowed by national legislation. By 1899 the by-laws on new building work were specifying such things as damp courses in houses, and convex road surfaces to allow rainwater to run off; and the process accelerated until in 1929 a new collection of regulations stipulated such things as the amount of air space to be enjoyed by occupants of lodging houses, and ordered that their windows should be open for two hours

65 High Wycombe Town Hall, seen here under refurbishment in the 1920s, replaced the Guildhall as the seat of local government in 1904.

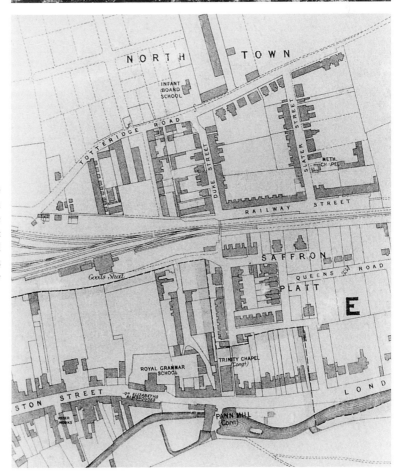

66 Saffron Platt, from the map prepared by the borough in 1880 to demonstrate the extension of the boundaries. It shows clearly how the town had already grown beyond its ancient limits: the old boundary is marked by the dotted line.

67   The first meeting of the council in its new chambers on Queen Victoria Road, 1932.

68   The water tower at Terriers, which gave its name to Tower Street, was built in 1911 and demolished in 1936. It formed an important element of the borough's water supply system which was gradually extended and improved at that time.

69   A great innovation in Wycombe in 1910 was the swimming baths in Frogmoor, opened by the entrepreneurial councillor Aleck Stacey and here photographed in 1912.

70 Building a new house along Benjamin Road in the 1890s. Locals collecting signatures for a petition here in the 1980s found residents born in Wales, Poland, Italy, Pakistan and St Vincent, and many of the large Victorian houses were by that time divided into flats.

each day 'unless reasonably prevented by the state of the weather'. In 1908 High Wycombe was the first town to adopt the Humane Slaughter of Animals provisions: by 1929, slaughterers were to make sure animals endured 'no unnecessary suffering or pain', and were not killed in the sight of other animals, or even where they could smell blood. The Electric Light and Power Company, established in 1898 on a site in Lily's Walk purchased from Lord Carrington, remained a private company, but even then Alderman Walter Birch sat on its Board so it was not entirely outside municipal influence.

Even in the areas over which the council chose not to extend its control, the voluntary organisations were becoming more structured as they realised that the old ways of managing were no longer adequate. In 1908 Miss Dove, Minnie Clarke (the town clerk's wife), the vicar's wife Mrs Shaw, and Mrs Read, established a mothers-and-babies clinic in Crown House; this in turn at length gave rise to the borough's Health Clinic on the Rye, opened in 1938, and, rather more quickly, to the Central Aid Society. The society was intended to co-ordinate the work of various charitable activities, such as the 'committees of ladies and others connected with the

various places of worship' who ran soup kitchens for the unemployed in the 1890s, or the Loan Blanket Society, which provided clean bedding for the poor from the 1840s until 1934. Probably the town's biggest voluntary organisation, the hospital, went from strength to strength on the basis of its thousands of subscribers, its fund-raising events, and the charity of the wealthy. In 1923 the Marquis of Lincolnshire made one of the Carrington family's most enduring gifts to the town by donating a new site for the hospital off Marlow Hill. The new 'War Memorial Hospital' was a thanksgiving to the area's war dead, and flourished for another quarter-century.

The same could hardly be said for the Free Library. This had been opened in 1876 by another great benefactor to the town, James Olliff Griffits, the self-educated saddler's son who became Recorder of the Borough of Reading and who was still energetic enough at 63 to marry a new wife of 29 and begin a second family! The Library was handed over to the council with great fanfare in 1882, but Griffits's stipulation that it should not receive support from the rates hobbled it for years. Cramped into its tiny building on Church Street, it was 'crippled by poverty'. Eventually

71 Despite being almost as far from the sea as it is possible to get in England, High Wycombe donated enough by way of charity to support a lifeboat, and celebrated in a parade in 1907.

72 Inside the War Memorial Hospital, as drawn by Francis Colmer in 1935.

73 A stall at a fund-raising event for the Free Library, held in the Abbey grounds in 1882. Mrs Kibbles and Mrs Phillips, who organised the stall, were both councillors' wives.

the council was compelled to alter the original trust deed and 'municipalised' the library, which suddenly became popular after its decision to start lending books. The absorption of such charitable institutions within the public realm was the shape of things to come. Still, a correspondent to *Bucks Interest* in 1955 recalled that even after the improvements the library was 'dimly lighted by a greenish gas; it smelt of all the dirty clothes of all the dirty children of long ago, and wet umbrellas', and, although

others disagreed with this assessment, the *Bucks Free Press* concurred: 'you crowded together on the dusty floor, peering short-sightedly at the titles in the dimness'.

Although the council was *doing* more and more, apart from the public works in the town centre it had had little impact on the built environment; but with Wycombe's expanding population and its own expanding view of what it could legitimately do, it was only a matter of time before this changed. 1913 was the crucial year. In January Mr Raffety announced that he would fund a prize for a competition to draw up Wycombe's first town plan to organise rationally the development of shops, factories, roads and all classes of housing. The plans that were entered were fairly superficial, although the winning entry, E.W. Turner's from Sheffield, did at least lay out a system of roads that respected the contours of the area rather than designing an impressive pattern that made no sense on the ground. The following month, the council declared it would build 16 cottages for rent at Wycombe Marsh, and by July plans for houses at Terriers were advanced enough to include the rent levels—from 4s. 9d. for a

two-bedroom house with living room and scullery, up to 8s. for one with four beds, scullery, living room and parlour. These plans were delayed by the First World War, but by 1920 the first hundred houses at Terriers had been built, and 94 at 'North Marsh'. This latter area soon acquired the nickname 'Tin Town' because of the steel frames of the houses. A third area of development was the West End Recreation Ground, donated by Lord Carrington in 1891, later used as a military training ground and finally becoming Wendover Street (its name a tribute to Viscount Wendover, the Carrington killed in the war) and Suffield Road.

74 The last day of the old library in Church Street, 1932, before the move to the present building. Now demolished, this was once the house of General Sir John Gaspard le Marchant, who founded the Royal Military Academy in the *Antelope Inn* on the High Street in 1799.

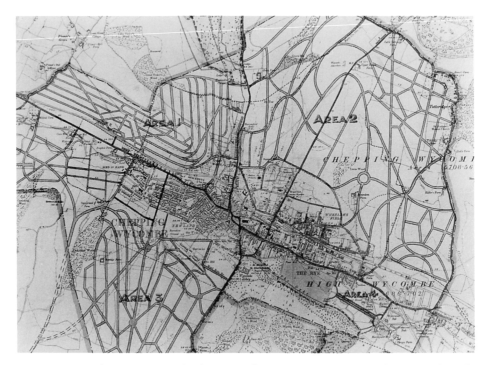

75   E.W. Turner's winning entry for the Town Plan competition, 1913. His design was the only one submitted which actually made some effort to respect the contour lines, and the suburbs as they eventually emerged were not entirely dissimilar.

76   The steel-framed construction of these 1921 council houses in Orchard Road, Wycombe Marsh, earned them the nickname of 'Tin Town'. Along with houses in Terriers, they were the council's first venture into public housing since the old corporation almshouses.

Private enterprise was not idle. Lord Carrington laid out Kitchener Road in the 1910s as artisans' housing while, after the war, the High Wycombe Furniture Trades Public Utility Society, a building society, paid for 30 houses for its members on Plumer Road. Development began in Micklefield when Mr Saunders of Range View Cottages in the Marsh bought a plot high above the track that led to Hicks Farm, and sold portions to his brother and sister, making room for three large family houses, 4 to 8 Micklefield Road. Mr J.K. Taylor, the Wycombe sweet-maker, built the first house in Hatters Lane above the railway line. He named it 'At Last'—the foundations had been laid in 1914 but the war and labour shortages intervened to delay its completion for years. Later, he sold the land for Kendalls Close. Despite all this activity, there was still an acute housing shortage into the 1930s. When in 1930 Francis Ching moved to Wycombe to begin working as a well-sinker for the Water Board, he slept rough in a shed at Pann Mill and then on a bench at the Easton Street pumphouse; then he went looking for a house for his family. These were few, and most houses with rooms for rent turned away children. Eventually Parker's, the solicitors, offered him a house in Crown Lane for £1 a week. It had a front room, parlour and kitchen and three bedrooms, although one was open to the rafters and unusable; there were also 'rats and mice galore' and he argued the rent down to 12s. The family eventually moved to Bowerdean for another 2s. 3d.

One feature that was still prominent in the local landscape was the allotment. Growing vegetables on allotments was an important way of easing the burden on working-class household finances, and the plots were everywhere. Olive Pearce's father, George Mealing, for instance, had an allotment at Bellfield 'so we had plenty of fresh vegetables'. The Carringtons were proud of the land they gave over to allotments; although the policy had begun as an electoral ploy, as R.H. Crewe admitted in 1874, later it became more obviously a charitable venture. In 1894 Lord Carrington told a public meeting at Tylers Green called to discuss smallholdings that his allotments of $1/10$th of an acre, established to offset the high price of vegetables, now numbered 1,100 and 'he was bound to say honestly that they had been a great success'. Gradually these areas began to be used for housing as people grew more prosperous and the allotment became more of a hobby than a necessity. Guinions Road was allotment land until its development in the 1930s, and 1934 saw the demise of the Bellfield and Bowerdean plots. By the 1960s, only Wycombe's new West Indian residents kept up the tradition in any substantial way, and even converted house gardens to horticulture in an effort to replicate the smallholdings they were familiar with from home. Mrs MacMillan of Desborough Avenue 'didn't seem to mind too much that her husband turned every square inch of earth into a vegetable patch ... it meant fewer visits to the grocer'.

The allotment was only one of the means of making ends meet. The Saunders family of Micklefield Road had enough ground to keep pigs and chickens and grow their own fruit and vegetables, and at least one 1930s house in Sands had a pigsty which is still extant. The river also provided some support, even though sources such as Sheahan's *Directory* of 1862 suggested that the bleaches from the paper mills had killed off all the fish, while the High Wycombe & District Angling Society disbanded in 1901, arguing that there were no fish left to be caught. This conflicts, however, with accounts of working-class households taking fish, and even crayfish, from the Wye well into the 1900s. Arthur Bradbury remembered catching crayfish in the stream along Oxford Road using tin cans thrown in from the neighbouring houses, and once he saw an 18-pound pike caught by a Mr Ball in the river and exhibited in a fish shop window.

In all these ways, the countryside still penetrated through this ostensibly industrial

77 The continuing import-
ance of the river: Albert Chaney
with a four-pound pike he
caught in The Dyke in 1936.

town, a situation symbolised by the right of all the borough's ratepayers to pasture cattle on the Rye. In the 1860s there had been up to sixty cattle on the meadow; by the 1920s there were only about thirty, but the dairies that owned them still sent cows down to the Hayward (sometimes under the supervision of the town's children) who closed the gate of the Rye behind them and then turned them out in the evening. He was supposed to lead them back to the Guildhall, but very often left them in Easton Street to amble their way home alone. Most of the time this presented little problem, although the occasional cow did find its way into a house or factory. However, with increasing traffic in the High Street, the practice came under the hostile scrutiny of the council and, realising that most of the cows were owned not by individual ratepayers but by dairies, it secured an Act of Parliament which came into force on New Year's Day, 1927, removing the ancient rights of pasturage from the town's citizens. From then on the Rye was nothing more than a public pleasure ground, and Wycombe's agricultural identity shrank even further.

Fifty years of modernisation were now moving towards a symbolic climax. A new

complex of neo-Classical buildings was built along one side of Crendon Street and continuing into Queen Victoria Road, to house, in the latter, a new library and council offices, which were finally opened in 1932. The new library was praised as 'a clear, light building, with an unfamiliar hospital-like efficiency'. Over subsequent years the suite was completed with the post office, which finally made the move from Easton Street to the site of the brewery; and the police station, a replacement for the building of 1815 in Newland Street, which had been denounced by the Police Review as 'the worst in the world'! These buildings shifted the whole balance of the town centre: its commercial core was still at the west end of the High Street, but that was now matched by an administrative base on the east, a new focal point for what had become an active, vigorous municipality.

High Wycombe had re-thought itself in those fifty years, but opinion was still sharply divided about it. In 1848 Henry Kingston had waxed very lyrical about the 'sequestered little spot' in its 'babble o' green fields', but a visitor a few years later found nothing to admire: 'it is a queer old place with nothing doing in it.

78   Crendon Street in the early 1900s, looking north towards Amersham Hill.

79   The children's paddling pool on the Rye, photographed here in 1930 with Rye Mill and Bassetsbury in the background, was followed a few years later by a municipal playground, and subsequently a miniature railway.

80   Wycombe sets out to defy the Depression: the inauguration of Shopping Week, 1931.

They have a few shops, but of course you can get nothing you want in them ... the stamp of dullness is on all.' The same range of views prevailed in the 1930s. In 1936 a visitor turned into the new Crendon Street after a long absence and 'thought for a moment that I'd got out at the wrong station'; although some pleasant buildings had been destroyed, he thought 'few would deny that the advantages gained were worth the price paid'. A little later, H. Hopkins wrote in *England Is Rich*, 'England is full of villages that grew up overnight; but few can have come through the experience so painlessly and, on the whole, pleasantly, as High Wycombe'. Less positively, Howard Marshall in *The Listener* described Wycombe as 'once a quiet old market town' and now 'rather like Brixton without the trams'. The west side of the town was 'a disgrace—a dreary hodge-podge of cheap building spread over the valley ... incredibly and stupidly ugly'. There were signs that the pace of change was beginning to

provoke a reactionary spirit. In 1933 former Mayor Harry Cox bequeathed a sum of money to the town to build a children's playground on the Rye, but when the council unveiled its plans, the irate residents of London Road condemned the playground as 'this miniature Wembley'!

Curiously, the climax of municipal independence and pride coincided with the beginning of the Depression. In an effort to promote the town's trade, 4-11 May 1931 was decreed to be Wycombe's first 'Shopping Week'. Huge crowds gathered to hear encouraging speeches at the Guildhall, strung across with a banner reading 'High Wycombe, the Furniture Town'. As the community faced the uncertainties of the future, that bland slogan seemed almost defiant. It was reticent but eloquent testimony to the pride Wycombe people felt in what they had achieved in the previous half-century. What the next would bring was beyond the imagination of anyone there.

Four

Clearance
(1932-1974)

In 1936 the *Bucks Free Press* profiled arguably the most powerful person in High Wycombe. He was not a councillor, nor the boss of a big furniture firm, but a reticent public official whose aim was to get on with his job with the least possible fuss. He was Lawrence Chadwick, then completing his 32nd year as Wycombe's Sanitary Inspector and in the process of having a decisive impact on the town's future development. From the Public Health Department's offices, first on Easton Street and then, from 1929, Town House in Castle Street, Chadwick regulated lodgings, refuse collection and water quality, inspected slaughterhouses and checked factory conditions and traders' weights and measures. From 1913, the testing of food and drugs was passed to him from the police. Even more of his work was carried out through persistent persuasion rather than legislation—in 1929, for instance, he managed to secure sanitary improvements in 21 of the town's pubs. Not for nothing did the *Free Press* state 'he enters into the daily lives of everyone who lives within the borough, in that he has to supervise ... the houses in which they live, their places of employment and of entertainment, and the food and drink which sustains them'.

The inspector's role in supervising the borough's housing stock would be of the greatest importance. He was already waging a campaign against sub-standard housing in the 1920s, particularly in the older areas west of the town centre. In 1929, 27 houses were condemned by his department and, apart from two cottages in Oakridge Road and Abbey Barn Road, all were in the old urban areas. As early as 1920, Chadwick had reported to the council that the western side of the town should be cleared of its houses wholesale and devoted to industrial use alone.

81 Lawrence Chadwick in 1955.

82   Joseph Sherriff (1856-1931) and his wife Clara, the owners of the restaurant in the High Street, photographed about 1890 with seven of their eight children. They were a typical middle-class family in old Wycombe.

The first focus of his attention was Newland. Although, as we have seen, some of the poorest houses there had already been absorbed into the spreading factories, it was still a cramped region of convoluted lanes and open ditches where almost two hundred houses had no mains drainage, and was viewed with loathing by other inhabitants. One remembered 'a horrible slum area' whose children 'used to go up and down White Hart Street poorly clad, often without knickers or shoes and always very dirty, hoping to find something to eat or an old coin in the gutter'. 'I wasn't very keen on going along there at all', said another. Wycombe's historian-librarian John Mayes saw it as 'so decrepit that even where good, decent

people fought hard against such an environment they were hard pressed to achieve even a moderate standard of living, and where people of less determination had given in to their surroundings the conditions were appalling'. The inspector's statistics told the same story. In 1929 he examined 58 houses in Spread Eagle Yard, Miller's Row and Newland Meadow, and in his opinion only one had 'good' closet arrangements, and another 'good' drains. In general, the condition of ten was 'moderate', but the rest were all defined as 'bad'. In some houses Chadwick found heavy-laden washing lines pulling rotten brickwork away from the outside walls. In contrast, when 288 houses in Saffron Platt and North Town were inspected in 1935, about a fifth were found to be 'good', and another third 'moderate'. Because, according to the inspector, Newland's subsoil was 'saturated with sewage', the water quality was atrocious for those properties not connected to the public main. 'I don't think I remember taking a sample of water from a tube well or pump that ever satisfied the test', Chadwick recalled.

Official opinion in the borough was coming round to accepting Chadwick's often-repeated strictures. Prompted by a string of state legislation such as the 1932 Town Planning Act, Wycombe had become 'slum-conscious and ashamed'. When, in 1935, the Council Health Committee received reports of areas where 162 people were crammed into one acre, where there was only one wash-house between six houses, and 'the only way to get ventilation ... was to take a pane of glass out', Cllr. Gibbs admitted, 'I was rather ashamed that Wycombe possessed such houses, and that there were Wycombe landlords who were prepared to charge rents' for them. It was not just purely sanitary considerations that weighed on the public conscience, either. Chadwick felt the 'moral side' was 'the most important factor in the whole problem' and the local Moral Welfare Association agreed that 'the clearance of slum areas is a big piece of moral welfare work'. Overcrowding, it was believed, led to 'immorality'—not just the spectre of incest, the dreadful thought at the back of the reformers' minds, but general brutalisation and crime.

Behind the urgent new emphasis placed on slum clearance was the ever-present shadow of the Depression. At Baker's, the veneer and marquetry suppliers, the signs of decline were already discernible in the late 1920s, and by 1932 the usual seasonal stagnation in the furniture trade had turned into severe industrial disruption, leaving 2,000 furniture makers out of work by the end of that year. As well as coping with its native unemployed, the town's reputation as a reliable source of work drew more unfortunates in from outside. At 9.30 in the morning, the temporary inmates of the Saunderton workhouse were turned out and 'walked into Wycombe in hordes'. Baker's took on a Mr Gorman from Compton's, the Ipswich organ makers, who had traipsed from town to town across southern England looking for cabinet work; and even this fine craftsman could only command a wage of 11d. an hour.

83 Wycombe's unemployed at the Malthouses, 1933.

The numbers in the dole queues were such that the Labour Exchange in Crendon Street opened a second office in the Christ Church Sunday School down the hill in Queen Victoria Road.

As far as it could, the town rallied round its unemployed and their families. In 1933, instead of holding its annual dinner at the *Red Lion*, the Furniture Manufacturers' Federation gave a Christmas party for the children whose fathers were out of work—'the Town Hall looked like a fairy palace', reported the *Free Press*. The old Malthouses formerly attached to Wheeler's Brewery, which stood behind the new library, were opened as a club for unemployed men in 1932, having been cleaned, heated, and fitted with furniture and games. One correspondent to the *Free Press* described it as 'a godsend to us unemployed'; while John Mayes found that 'a visit there always left the visitor confused between depression at the dreary surroundings and elation at the wonderful spirit'. Concerted efforts were also begun to re-invigorate the town's trade. The annual 'Shopping Week' was started in 1931 and by 1932 had become 'Furniture Month'. A year

later, 42 manufacturers staged exhibitions of their wares and invited buyers from across the country, and the buyers were reciprocating by 1936 when Whiteleys of London held a 'Wycombe Fortnight'. Nonetheless, despite the *Free Press* finding 'evidence of progress and prosperity on all sides' in 1936, the situation did not improve permanently until the Second World War. Alfred Saunders of the Marsh, for instance, a chair-maker at Gibson's in Temple End, never worked a full day from about 1930 until war broke out, and he was far from alone.

It may have been these stresses that prompted the big employers to adopt more paternalistic habits. Castle Brothers was the first furniture firm to begin an employee pension scheme in 1934, and in that year also took its workers on a summer day trip to Barry Island. Keen's workforce went away every September to resorts such as Southend and Brighton. This began a tradition which continued until recent years: Ercol's last day trip to Bournemouth took place in the early 1990s, by which time it had become both costly and, because of all sorts of social change, superfluous. The furniture

84   Shops at Temple End in 1960. These, and the 1905 railway viaduct visible in the background, were demolished in 1990.

85 Workers at Styles & Mealing's furniture factory in Ogilvie Road gather for their annual outing, 1946.

86 Thomas Burch Ford (d.1900), Victorian paper master, the owner of Snakeley Mills in Loudwater from about 1860. Ford's was an innovation in social provision for its workers.

87 Westbourne Street Methodist Church's Slate & Loan Club Christmas share-out in 1935—an annual event which affected hundreds of families across the town.

workers were not alone, as in July 1934 Loudwater was reported to be 'a deserted village' because most of the population was in Margate courtesy of the paper-master Mr Ford of Snakeley Mill. By 1935 Gomme's had purchased Redford's Sports Ground at Terriers as a venue for annual entertainments for its workers: a thousand people attended the first such event, to enjoy amusements like 'knocking the old man's hat off, Mr Clarke being the target', and bowling for a pig, which attracted 'a big trade'.

Once upon a time these services would have been provided by, or at least through, the churches, but new secular institutions and occasions were a sign that the hold of church and chapel was loosening. The Wycombe Infants Welfare Centre began day trips to Southsea for children, mirroring the chair-masters' provisions for their parents—outings which the old Sunday School Treats could hardly compete with. At a more local level there were secularised versions of the Treats such as the Bowerdean Children's Picnic in Totteridge Woods which provided for a thousand children. The chapel savings clubs, known as 'slate clubs', which had been vital in providing

working-class families with small loans and payments for costs like medical bills, were still powerful. The Westbourne Street Methodist Slate & Loan Club, for instance, was the largest such group in the county with a membership that ran into thousands, and 'joining this club was essential for working-class lads as they left school'. That would become less and less true as the support it offered was increasingly provided by employers, the council and the state. The old chapel-going Sabbatarianism was also ebbing away. In the 1890s the police had solemnly confiscated balls and goalposts if men were caught playing football on the Rye on Sundays; 40 years later, the sturdy old Nonconformist Caleb Bridger, the Easton Street shoemaker, complained that the Sabbath had been utterly disrespected since the First World War. 'We had to fight on Sundays out there,' was the attitude he found: 'Why should we be any different now?' Betting was still illegal, but the council decided that it could do little about the greyhound racing track that sprang up at Sawpit Hill in Hazlemere in the mid-1930s. What would have caused horror just twenty years before was now in receipt of the official blind eye.

One new form of entertainment, in particular, had beaten the chapels for the allegiance of the young. High Wycombe's first cinema, the Palace in Frogmoor, symbolically opened in a vacated Primitive Methodist Chapel in 1909 before burning down in 1912 and being replaced by the Electroscope. The Grand opened the following year in Desborough Road, followed by another Palace in Frogmoor in 1922, the Majestic (later the Odeon) in Castle Street in 1930, and the Rex, Oxford Street, in 1937. Between then and 1962, when the Grand closed, the town had four picture houses; and they became a central part of growing up as the Saturday morning cinema visit turned into an unmissable ritual after the Second World War. The Odeon, for instance, as one of the big circuit cinemas, ran a Saturday club for seven to 15-year-olds which boasted 1,250 members in 1951.

The opening of new cinemas showed that, even in the 1930s, there was still some money about to spare, in contrast to the deep impoverishment suffered by many before the First World War. Home chair-caning, which had a place in so many people's recollections, had been the top rung on the ladder of ways to make ends meet. It was better than collecting leftover fruit and vegetables from the market to sell, or selling dung collected at the cattle

88 High Wycombe's (and Buckinghamshire's) earliest cinema, the Palace, took over this former Primitive Methodist chapel in 1909, beside Aleck Stacey's swimming baths. It lasted only until 1912 when the building was gutted by fire, and then it reopened on the opposite side of the road.

89   Desborough Road in the early 1900s, looking eastward towards the Desborough Road Schools, built in 1888 on the corner with Desborough Avenue.

market, or hawking 'odds and ends' from a pram like 'Oxo Ada' of Duke Street, or any of a hundred other disagreeable ways to make a penny. Every pleasure then had been hard-won. The Bradburies of George Street certainly enjoyed their treat of fish and chips whenever the slate club paid out, but that showed how rare it was; and Mrs Bradbury was usually paying back the grocer until August for the food the family ate at Christmas. There would still be hardship—the unpaid week's holiday in August was enough of a strain to be 'dreaded' by chair workers, down-and-outs like 'Old Chaney' would carry on sleeping under a tent of coats in the hedge at Hicks Farm, and 'Soapy Atkins' the tramp and his cat would still freeze to death in an allotment shed in 1947—but there would be no return to pre-First World War levels of poverty. Even the health of the borough had improved. When he retired as Medical Officer

in 1935, Dr Bannerman noted with satisfaction that the previous 24 years had seen typhus eliminated, the capacity of the water system rise tenfold, and the infantile death rate cut by nearly two-thirds.

General improvement, then, made the slums look more and more a disgrace; short-term hardship made the problem more urgent; and the shift away from voluntary organisations like churches convinced the council that it was its responsibility to act. The first round of slum clearance areas, announced in 1932, covered Newland Meadow, Miller's Row, Collins Row (where 'the houses are by reason of repair and sanitary defects unfit for human habitation'), Mendy Street, Newland Street, Mellett's Yard, Rosa Place and Bowdery's Lane. The conditions in Newland were so notorious that there was little opposition, although even here the demolitions did not go uncontested.

Mrs Essex of 5 Beckford's Yard complained, 'I don't want a council house. I have lived in that house for 48 years and it is not damp. I keep it in very good condition ... I can't afford to pay a lot of money out of a 10-shilling pension'. These were fair points. Mrs Gillett's mother, for instance, struggling to raise a family alone, could not afford the council rents and had to move into rooms after their home was condemned, before occupying another old house elsewhere in the town. Other householders kept their properties well. The Granges at 25 Mendy Street had 'a tiny front garden with the sunflowers blazing in the corner, a window box with geraniums', as their granddaughter recalled.

But things were to get much stickier for the clearance campaign. In 1935, when 233 houses had been pulled down and 704 people re-housed, the council declared another 14 clearance areas, this time in Frogmoor, St Mary Street, and five in Wycombe Marsh. The last nobody objected to—Alderman Vernon had described Marsh as 'a disgrace to civilisation' in 1901—but the proposed demolitions in the town centre ran up against articulate interests. The sanitary inspector's methods and motivations were put under scrutiny in a public enquiry in 1936. The corporation side held its nerve: Mr Chadwick maintained that the *Horse & Jockey* pub was 'putrid' and the council solicitor argued that the ceilings of houses along

90 Once called 'The Canal', Frogmoor has been redeveloped several times in the last 250 years, most recently in 2002. The fountain was erected in 1875 and controversially removed during the Second World War, though whether for scrap or because it had become an eyesore depends on which story you believe. This view is from the 1920s.

91 Developing town: a view of Frogmoor in the late 1920s, complete with fountain, telegraph pole, bus, and public loos.

92 Employees of the Thames Valley Bus Company in the 1950s, probably at the depot at Wycombe Marsh.

the Oxford Road were 'sodden with filth'. Against this, the appellant lawyers took apart the criticisms of the properties line by line, suggesting that sills were capable of repair, or that landlords had already replaced rotten brick-work since the inspector's visit. Mr Covell thought that the cottages called Sunnybank on Oxford Road were 'decidedly attractive', while Mr Winter-Taylor visited St Mary Street and 'was struck by the houses I saw there, and the pride the occupiers showed in their homes ... the *Horse & Jockey* is one of the best examples of a beer shop in the district, and to say it is a slum is absurd'. Chadwick's reports were 'exaggerated', he said. John Hudson, a carver at no.33 who had a workshop in the garden, felt the inspector's remarks were 'an insult' to

93 Remington Terrace along the Oxford Road in 1960, at the Bridge Street corner. This photograph shows the river Wye still open: during the redevelopments of the 1960s it was decided that incorporating it into the new arrangements would be too expensive, and it was culverted under the town centre.

him and his wife. Some of the reformers' statements certainly gave the more decent inhabitants cause for resentment. Lawrence Chadwick had already written in an official report that 'one can hardly blame a person for not knowing the value of cleanliness, fresh air and sunlight, who has spent his days in a squalid court'. Now his colleague Dr Moore, the medical officer, opined to much controversy that occupiers were often so debased by their surroundings that they were 'not capable of understanding good conditions'. Finally, the curator of the Museum, Fred Skull, was roped in to compare St Mary Street with West Wycombe village, and state that the demolition of the cottages would 'verge on a public scandal'. Most of these buildings avoided the bulldozer for another 30 years.

Where were the former slum residents going to live, especially when there was so much pressure on the available housing? In fact, even Lawrence Chadwick took pride in the high proportion of modern properties in Wycombe's housing stock. Many of these were private developments. Rupert Stevens, High Wycombe's big butcher, farmer and horse dealer, bought four plots at Gillett's Farm in the 1920s at 3s. 6d. perpetual ground rent from Sir John Dashwood and built eight houses on

94 One of the great treasures of Wycombe's archives—though not perhaps always an uplifting one—is the collection of photographs taken by the Public Health Department before the demolitions of the 1930s. This is Janes Court off St Mary Street, probably built by the Janes family of chair-makers. (Illustrations 94-98 are all from the slum clearance archive.)

95 Backs of houses in The Quicks, Wycombe Marsh.

96   Millers Row, Newland, with Birch's factory in the background.

97   Spread Eagle Court, off Newland Street.

98 Backyard behind Nos. 1 and 8 Newland Street.

99 Railway Place led from the rear of Station Road to London Road down the side of Trinity United Reform Church; here it is photographed in the 1940s. Demolition began in 1964.

the land which he sold at £110 profit apiece, and he was typical of innumerable small developers; but about 93 per cent of the Newland people went into housing provided by the borough council. First in Castlefield, where the long valley-bottom roads stretched south from the brooding ramparts of Desborough Castle, and then in Micklefield: the new suburbs of three-bed corporation semis paralleled a housing boom which was taking place all across the land.

For those who could not afford the costs of removal—and there were many—council vehicles were used to ferry belongings up from the valley floor to the hills. Whatever their misgivings had been before moving, there was nothing but praise from the new residents of Spearing Road. 'We have been given houses of which we can be proud', Mrs Judd told the *Free Press*. 'The air makes all the difference. Just to be here makes me feel better.' 'It's like coming out of a prison,' agreed Mrs King a

100   Castlefield estate being built, early 1930s.

101   Builder's advert for new houses in Micklefield, 1934.

102 The *Half Moon*, Oxford Road, drawn by Francis Colmer in 1929. This pub moved to Dashwood Avenue in 1934.

few doors away. The clearances were 'a wonderful kindness ... the best thing that ever happened, with light airy rooms, a garden and shed, the great luxury of a bathroom and electricity, and the fresh air was a joy.'

Following the precedent of the 1880s and 1890s, facilities moved where the people did. In the case of pubs, this was again a deliberate campaign on the part of the sanitary inspector and the licensing authorities. In 1933 the *Morning Star* on Totteridge Road was closed and moved a quarter-mile to Bowerdean, 'where there has sprung up a miniature town', while the *Half Moon* in Oxford Road was earmarked for relocation to the western suburbs where 'workers ... need a new public house'. It moved to its new Desborough Park Road site the following year. Sands was important enough a growth area for the justices to consider transferring Newland's little *Mason's Arms* there, while Colonel Briggs of Benskins brewery offered to close the *Jolly Butcher* if they could move the *Golden Fleece* westwards too (in the

event, many years later, it went east to Hatters Lane). The Church of England, conversely, withdrew from Sands, replacing the village's little tin church of St Mary with the far grander Byzantine pile of Our Lady and St George's, whose first stage was consecrated in 1936 and completed with a huge copper dome two years later. It perched on the hilltop below Desborough Castle, dominating the new estates. By 1937 it was looking out over the County Secondary School on Mill End Road, the town's biggest school since the new Royal Grammar, including gymnasia, halls, canteen and staff rooms. Mill End was followed two years later by junior schools in Castlefield.

The map on page 90 shows how the developments of the 1930s altered High Wycombe's whole topography. Whereas earlier growth had occupied the valley floor and pushed out along the main roads, the new estates ran up the valleys to the hilltops of Cressex, Downley and Terriers, and in fact defined the shape the town would take. Later

103   Bowerdean in the early 1930s, with the few remaining buildings of Bowerdean Farm on the left and Totteridge Hill on the right, leading up towards the old hamlet of Totteridge, which was soon to be enveloped by the spreading town. At the top left is St Francis's Church, Terriers, built in 1930.

development would do little more than fill in this outline. The old village communities of Booker, Downley, Sands, Terriers, Totteridge and Marsh suddenly found themselves incorporated within the town which had previously been a barely-connected entity. In 1933 the *Free Press* noticed the 'bungaloid growths which have recently staked a claim to Booker's rurality'. Over the years this led to an increasing sense of nostalgia for 'village life', especially when a once-crucial organisation closed and provoked a bout of soul-searching. The web of connections such an institution could build up was obvious. Sands Methodist Church, for example, closed in 1982: its last funeral was of Caroline Stallwood, a grand-daughter of one of the founder members, while the last baptism (on the same day) was that of one of her own great-granddaughters. On the other hand, some of the old communities were invigorated, or

even transformed. 'Cressex' had been just a geographical expression until the 1930s, but by 1962 it was 'a little shopping centre', with its own pub, the *Turnpike* (Simonds Breweries of Reading had wanted to call it the *Jolly Sandboy* until local protestors demanded a more relevant name). Later the area acquired a community centre. By 1972 Downley had gained a variety of shops, 'a complete contrast to Downley as it was years ago, when it consisted of just a group of brick and flint cottages, a farm and two pubs'.

What this expansion represented was a sudden transformation of the landscape from the rural hinterland of a small industrial town into a two-mile belt of suburbs. Wycombe's old agricultural identity, symbolically relinquished with the depasturage of the Rye in 1927, now withered away entirely as agricultural businesses amalgamated or closed. The High

104 St Mary and St George's, newly completed in 1938. The copper dome oxidised and the white paint wore away, but the building has remained a striking landmark.

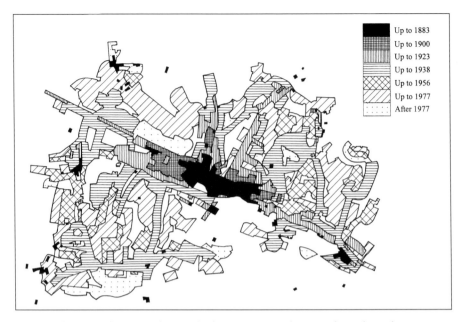

Legend:
- Up to 1883
- Up to 1900
- Up to 1923
- Up to 1938
- Up to 1956
- Up to 1977
- After 1977

105 High Wycombe's growth over the last 120 years. This map shows how the town was originally clustered in the valley bottom; how until the 1920s growth extended mainly along the axial roads; how the 1930s estates claimed the hilltops and defined the outline of the town; and how that outline was filled in during later decades.

106 Sands in the 1920s, from Mill End Road. Gallows Lane runs up to Chapel Lane in the centre of the photograph. Sands, like the other hamlets around Wycombe, was an entirely distinct community before improvements to roads and new housing joined it to the town from the 1930s onwards.

107 Children at Copyground Farm, 1924. Farming came to an end here by 1930 and the buildings were converted to light industrial uses (including chair-making). The 18th-century farmhouse still stands, now surrounded by modern development.

Wycombe Corporation Act of 1946 extinguished common rights in Kingsmead, Keep Hill and Marsh Green, turning them into public pleasure grounds like the Rye, and ten years later the owners of Funges Farm stopped putting their cows out on Holywell Mead after the swimming pool was built. Around the same time, Associated Dairies was formed on the Cressex industrial estate from five local dairies across the town, and in Hazlemere to the north the farmers of Hill, Oakengrove and Manor Farms applied for permission to build 600 houses on their land—at 109 acres between them, the farms were no longer viable. Green Farm was demolished in 1971, the same year as the final demise of Pann Mill. This, the oldest surviving

mill in the town, had produced animal feed for many years, but in 1967 the owners announced their intention to build offices on the site. The council for its part considered using it for 'a suitable civic building' but in the end the land was left derelict. The agricultural elements of the fair, revived in 1947 after a gap of nine years and soon renamed the Wycombe Show, shrank until only a few pens of animals survived—more a marketing exercise than a market. The weekly Cattle Market itself was now seen as a nuisance, and the 1952 town plan envisaged it moving to Sands, a plan strongly opposed by the National Farmers Union, the Chamber of Commerce and local butchers who pointed to the lack of facilities

108 Wycombe Show, 1951. The weather wasn't always better then!

109 Yards to the rear of Brook Street in 1955, before its demolition in the second wave of slum clearances.

there. The market's turnover was still £187,000 in 1962, but five years later it came to an end, and with it the town's last significant agricultural link. The council's Conservative opposition promised the NFU that they would revive it if they won the elections, but never did.

The clearances halted after 1936, but this did not mean the perceived problems had gone away. Lawrence Chadwick had always believed that the west end of the town was 'far too valuable for small cottage properties', and the post-war town plan concurred with his aim 'to have cleared the lot from Newland to Desborough Avenue'. It took only a gentle legislative nudge, and rising expectations of what a decent house should provide, to begin the clearances again. The 1954 Housing Repairs and Rents Act required local authorities to draw up lists of houses for demolition or improvement: and an increased view of the scope of public authority, 1950s progressive optimism, and Compulsory Purchase Orders would make things that much easier.

No.1 Clearance Area was Brook Street, a road of terraced mid-Victorian cottages just north-west of Newland: demolition began in

1955 and by the end of 1956 only three families remained, but this was just a toe in the water. In the 1930s St Mary Street had escaped destruction, but now Cllr Sidney Goulbourn, Chairman of the Planning Committee, declared that it and Lily's Walk had 'no possibility of being repaired and no historic or aesthetic value'. The plans were unanimously adopted by the council. They would, enthused the *Free Press*, 'change the face of Wycombe'. Indeed they would. By 1957, 1,408 Wycombe houses were deemed unfit to live in: this meant that the next 17 years would see the clearances of the 1930s increase more than fourfold. The 'west end' roads—Short, Baker, George, and Richardson Streets —were the first to disappear, and in the event the demolitions extended beyond even the point Chadwick had envisaged. The first clearances on the east side, four

houses in Duke Street, came in 1961, and by the end of the 1960s over thirty houses in Bowerdean Road and the little roads at the edge of the Rye, Park and Kent Streets, had been included. By the time the programme came to an end in 1974, much of Wycombe had undergone radical change.

Many residents welcomed the changes, although others feared a move away from familiar shops, pubs and other facilities. Officially-stated objections, as voiced at a 1968 enquiry into one of the purchase orders, echoed those made 30 years before—the council's criticisms of houses were said to be 'exaggerated' and the scheme arguably represented a chance for it to acquire large areas of land at a fraction of the market rate. 'It's a damn lot of lies', was Bert Stallwood of 19 Duke Street's verdict on the inspector's report into Saffron Platt

110   Bridge Street looking towards Oxford Road in 1960.

111   Marsh Mill decorated for Queen Elizabeth's Coronation in 1953.

properties in 1970; 'Nothing but a land grab', agreed his neighbour Albert Belcher. Shop-keepers like the Sherlocks, whose corner shop stood at the end of Temple Street until 1961, took some levering out. But theirs were marginal voices, and few were raised in their support—at least for the moment.

What was the true story? It was certainly the case that the slum clearance campaign help-fully coincided with the schemes to rebuild the town centre, but the subsequent fate of the cleared streets suggested there was no council 'master plan' at all. They ended up a mixture of car parks, light industrial units and flats. Professional opinion among architects, planners and public health officials alike was that, where some properties in a street were sub-standard, it was more efficient to pull them all down and rebuild. Wycombe was simply swept along by the same enthusiasm.

In the early 1900s, the High Street iron-monger's, Davenport Vernon, took the bold step of converting to a motor garage, a small sign of things to come. Just before the First World War there were races on Sunday

mornings from the Desborough Park Road milestone to the top of Old Dashwood Hill in which up to 20 vehicles would take part, but increasing traffic meant such high-jinks could hardly last. Soon eastward traffic came bombing along West Wycombe Road in greater and greater volumes, only to meet the twists and dog-legs of the town centre. One correspondent to the *Bucks Free Press* in 1933 told how he had seen Oxford Road 'change from a quiet country road to a sort of speed-hog paradise' with noisy, speeding lorries, and buses 'racing each other'! From 1930 various steps were taken to improve traffic flow. The camber from Oakridge Road into Oxford Road, so steep that passing buses heeled over, was levelled out, and the *Black Boy* pub which jutted into Church Street next to the churchyard was demolished, serendip-itously revealing 'the beauty of the old church tower' (the licence was moved to a new *Black Boy* in Terriers). The *Roundabout* pub was moved from the corner of Bridge Street so that a dangerous junction could be rounded off; the bend outside Marsh Mills where six people had been killed in seven years was levelled out; and in 1936 Marlow Hill was straightened and Crendon Lane was widened and rebuilt with the removal of most of its old buildings. In 1934 Wycombe's first traffic lights replaced the bobbies on duty at the Guildhall corner, followed next year by an urban speed limit and the first speeding conviction when Mr Harris, a Paddington builder, was caught by the police on the London Road at Loudwater.

This was just tinkering, however, and more action was needed. As early as 1935 the council had drawn up a scheme to drive a new road 'through Newland' to link Oxford Road with the High Street, and this, in modified form, emerged in post-war plans. In 1947, Tudor houses in White Hart Street were actually pulled down to make way for it. A.M. Chitty's draft development plan of 1950

identified traffic as one of Wycombe's major problems. He advised first widening Oxford Road, then creating an Inner Relief Road to bypass the town centre; the building of an Outer Relief Road, taking traffic past the town entirely, was to be left to the Ministry of Transport.

The truth was that the Oxford-London road, which had brought Wycombe so much prosperity over the centuries, was now becoming a menace to its well-being. By the late 1950s jams in the High Street were frequent, not surprising on days when cars were parked three deep along it. Travellers between the capital and the university city now had to allow an hour of their journey simply to get through High Wycombe. West Wycombe was 'almost unliveable in' and the Dashwoods were

112   Marlow Hill before being straightened out in 1936.

113   Crendon Street before the road-widening scheme of 1936. The new buildings on the western side have already been built, curving behind the old ones. The eastern side did not disappear for many years.

kept awake by 'fearful screeches all through the night' coming from its High Street.

Only a radical solution would be adequate. The County Planning Officer, F.B. Pooley, was haunted by the experience of American city centres, bisected and effectively destroyed by huge roads, and wanted to save Wycombe from a similar fate, by keeping people and traffic apart and raising the relief road on a flyover with shops beneath. Shopkeepers vigorously protested in the belief that the road would take trade from the town, while the Rye Protection Society, under the leadership of Jack Scruton, successfully prevented it from clipping the edge of that ancient meadow. Sidney Goulbourn nonetheless spoke for the majority at the opening of Abbey Way in 1967 when he called it 'the first part of a dream come true', a dream completed three years later when the eastern half opened. The motorway was developed at the same time; here, protest centred on the

impact it would have east of Wycombe and the planned cutting through the Chiltern escarpment to the west. The people of Loudwater, enraged at the proposed 'murder of a village', did manage to get the route of the cross-valley viaduct diverted, but protest marches against the 'gash on the skyline' at Stokenchurch proved fruitless; the Wycombe bypass opened in 1970 and the cutting went through a couple of years later. Residents and businesses were, generally, delighted with their safer streets and easier means of getting into, out of, and through the town. 'It's brought High Wycombe alive', said the manager of Sainsbury's.

Only the north-south route was not tackled. To avoid traffic funnelling down Amersham Hill, and the consequent accidents as runaway lorries smashed into the central cross-roads, would mean cutting new roads or upgrading existing ones, but every scheme came

114 The new traffic management plan for the town centre, as unveiled in 1934.

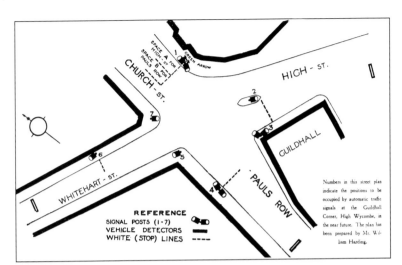

115 The Loudwater Viaduct, built to carry the M40, under construction in March 1968.

116 The cottages in the centre here, dwarfed by the college building, and others reached through the archway, were built by John Holland in the early 1850s and named Holland's Yard. The Carrington estate bought them in the 1880s and renamed them Lily's Walk after one of the Carrington daughters. They were demolished in 1959.

117 The site of the Octagon, 1967.

to grief. Between 1970 and 1975, and again in 1988, the council proposed a relief road up Hughenden Valley to join Hazlemere with Frog-moor; on both occasions protest overwhelmed the plan and the authorities had to be content with improving bottlenecks here and there.

Traffic relief was only one aspect of whole-sale redevelopment. To an extent this had already begun with the two modernist buildings that now towered over the town centre, the new college (1955-6) and the hospital (1961-6). In his planner's crystal ball Fred Pooley saw that 'people shop more and more by car. They want safety and convenience', and the local authori-ties set about providing it. The clearance programme included some properties west of the Guildhall cryptically called the 'Central Area': this was to be the site of the Octagon, Wycombe's version of the covered shopping centres which were being acquired by most late-1960s towns

in Britain. The borough architect provided the design; Sainsbury's moved in; Murray's, Wycombe's home-grown department store, took the opportunity to expand its area to 70,000 square feet. When the Duchess of Kent opened the centre, together with its car parks, in 1970 the mayor, the Rev. John Skipp, described how it had 'brought the 20th century into the heart of High Wycombe without destroying its soul'. By now old buildings were perishing at a hectic rate, and some only just survived. In 1963 the High Wycombe Arts Association stated that the *Red Lion Hotel* had 'no special architectural merit' (although Fred Pooley put a preservation order on it), and a public meeting of local residents decided that the Guildhall itself was 'an ugly structure devoid of any beauty' and argued that it should be demolished to ease traffic flow. It was not until 1969 that these suggestions were finally scotched.

118 Planners attempted to ensure that Wycombe's new suburbs had a chance of developing into organic communities by providing local parades of shops, such as these in Gayhurst Road, photographed in the 1970s.

By the mid-1970s the dust began to settle. When, in 1965, Jack Scruton had bitterly told the Parliamentary Committee examining the relief road proposal that 'the lovely town we once knew has gone. If it were not for the Rye it could be Ealing, Acton or Shepherd's Bush', he was an eccentric. Ten years on, the townspeople suddenly realised that clearance, roadbuilding and redevelopment had produced a Wycombe totally different from the cramped, familiar little 'Furniture Town' of thirty years before. The reaction was violent and the natural response was to blame the planners for decisions in which the whole town had taken part or acquiesced. The gap which had once been the despised Newland was now referred to as the 'Western Desert'. One writer saw in the changes only 'a series of muddled attempts to "bring the town into the 20th century", as planners are so fond of saying'. In 1978 the *Free Press* launched an editorial attack on the 'Tatty Town' whose creation, ironically, it had supported, its 'depressing picture of change and decay, of rubbish and ruin'. Questioned in 1980, District Planning Officer Malcolm Dean admitted that some of the clearances had been 'regrettable': from now on the council would improve areas rather than demolish them, beginning with Green Street and later taking in Saffron Platt, North Town, and Hughenden Road. By the mid-1990s, a series of decisions that were well-intentioned and had near-universal support were remembered as 'the peacetime Blitz of the 1960s that tore the heart out of the town'. It was an ambiguous legacy.

Five

New Communities
(1935–2000)

People had always come to Wycombe: the diversity and transience of the population, for good and ill, made it what it was. Flemish weavers, for instance, repeatedly took advantage of special terms introduced in the 14th century by the Common Council to encourage the cloth trade, and this tradition persisted. In the 1850s the town boasted cosmopolitan citizens such as the watchmakers, Italian Benjamin Carrori in Newland and the German Joseph Feuerbach in the High Street. In the 20th century, Wycombe's capacity for importing vigour and re-inventing itself was to be proved yet again.

The harsh conditions of the Depression set large numbers of people on the move. It was natural for the jobless to gravitate towards London, and coming along the road or railway from south Wales towards the Capital brought you, incidentally, to High Wycombe. Many of the Welsh visitors stayed and, willing as they were to work for less than the native craftsmen, their presence was not always welcomed. 'If you can't speak Welsh you can't get a job', locals grumbled, although some immigrants did not notice any friction—in 1933 'Taff' of Sands told the *Free Press* that he had been 'treated with the greatest respect and kindness'. Only future census publications will give a clear picture of the Welsh influx, but it must have been substantial. The original estate in Micklefield was colloquially known as 'Rhonddha Valley' because of its Welsh

population, while in the 1940s the High Wycombe & District Wales Society organised annual 'Get Togethers' on St David's Day that were attended by hundreds. One immigrant, Wyn Elias from Abergwyanfi, achieved a level of fame in the 1950s as Lucille Graham, a regular TV and radio singer. She and her family had performed as 'The Ten Welsh Singers' at Oakridge Baptist Church.

War was to be an agent of even greater change. In the first place, Wycombe acquired a significant military identity. Hughenden Manor became a reconnaissance and map-making centre, and Bomber Command moved in at Naphill a few miles away. The civil airfield at Booker closed in July 1939 and reopened two years later to train pilots for the Fleet Air Arm in 72 Tiger Moths. Most obviously of all, the Americans arrived. In 1942, the headmistress of Wycombe Abbey School received an official notice that in 13 days' time the girls would have to vacate the site to make way first for 8th Bomber Command, then for the USAF's 8th Army Force; they did not return until May 1946, reassembling after dispersal throughout the country. Pubs such as the *Flint Cottage*, which had a 'Yanks' Bar' at the back, were favourites with the US servicemen (partly because the Cottage was easy to find: straight down the hill from the Abbey and up the other side!), and for two years until 1945 Wycombe was the only town in England with an Anglo-American Services Club, staffed by the YMCA.

119   The Welsh Society meet for their annual dinner in 1957.

Eventually the Americans left the Abbey but stayed at their Daws Hill base, which would become the focus of peace marches in the 1960s and 1980s. In 1982, 2000 protesters marched from Naphill to Daws Hill and set up a 'peace camp': the protests carried on every year until the end of the Cold War.

The Americans were transitory residents: others came to stay. When Poland found itself in the Soviet sphere of influence after the war, thousands of refugees and servicemen in the Free Polish forces had to choose between living under their traditional enemies in a Communist state, or beginning a new life elsewhere—in many cases, in Britain and specifically in south Bucks. The number of Poles in Wycombe was less than those who went north to Amersham, but they were a persistent minority, if not a very self-assertive one (the Polish Club opened in Micklefield only in 1972). Individuals such

as the Wycombe Wanderers player Henryk Wergzyk, dubbed 'the Flying Pole' by the *Free Press*, kept the community in the public eye.

Wartime immigrants from closer to home were more significant. Despite the military presence, the Government—with some justification, as it turned out, for Wycombe was never bombed—designated the town a 'safe area'. The first evacuees from London arrived in 1940, and were put up in churches before being settled around the town. Other new residents were not evacuees as such, but commuters who stayed in Wycombe homes and worked in London during the day, so that 'every house was crammed right full'. The Clarkes in Spring Gardens had lodgers in the front room and back bedroom, people like the Tewgroths who worked at the Swedish Embassy, or the Browns who were civil servants. Organisations sought the safety of Wycombe as well as individuals.

120   Henryk Wergzyck as shown in a *Free Press* cartoon in 1947.

121   Wycombe's Area 7 Home Guard unit, 1940. On the right of the second row is the photographer, Cyril Roberts.

122   Evacuees from London enjoy a Christmas Party provided at the Union Baptist Church Rest Centre on Easton Street, 1941.

A Hammersmith school relocated to Spring Gardens School and shared it with the natives, using the building in the mornings, and it was followed by the Chiswick Girls' School. The girls of the Shoreditch Technical College moved into one half of The Limes on Easton Street in 1939, then occupied the whole building after the Conservatives moved out. It was the same story at Wycombe High School, whose pupils and those of the Ealing Girls' High School swapped to and fro between the school and the Union Baptist Church Hall.

Hundreds of these incomers looked at the town they had moved to, and liked it enough to stay. At the *Hour Glass* pub in Sands, for instance, the landlord, William Ferguson, was a Scot who had come to Wycombe with the RAF in 1941, while his wife had come from Finsbury when her parents' pub was bombed

and the family relocated to the *White Horse* on West Wycombe Road. The pub's windows were cleaned by Herbert Chalk who had been born in Edmonton. This process carried on long after the war, as the capital's families came to look for 'their own home in the country, away from the hustle and bustle of London'.

The First World War had diversified High Wycombe's industrial base in a limited way. In 1917 the furniture manufacturers Birch & Cox, Cecil Smith, Skull, and Gomme set up the Wycombe Aircraft Company, but although it never made a single plane its factories provided a home for two London businesses, Gilford Motors of Holloway Road and later the stamp-makers Harrisons. This foreshadowed the greater impact of the Second World War: with Wycombe declared safe for industry as well as people, dozens of the capital's companies came

123 Mr H. Cutler (1894-1963), tutor in design at the college, as shown in a caricature by Reg Trundle. Through his students, Mr Cutler was a strong influence on many of the town's furniture makers, and was recruited during the Second World War to help design the official Utility range. He was given the MBE in 1953 for services to education.

124 Spring Gardens School, one of the new suburban schools built between 1890 and the First World War as Wycombe expanded outwards. Here, the pupils are gathered in 1910 a year after the school's opening.

125 During the First World War many furniture factories went over to munitions production, and propellers were a common product, constructed from numerous sheets of thin wood glued together. The identity of the company shown in this photograph, though, is not known.

west. Long & Hambly of Highgate came to Wycombe in 1942 to manufacture gas masks and valves before moving on to make rubber mouldings. Cossor's, makers of radar screens and cathode tubes, moved to Kingsmead under the aegis of the Ministry of Aircraft Production, which bought land there in 1941 and requisitioned more under the 1946 Corporation Act. Aircraft manufacture played a special role in changing the High Wycombe economy. Dancer & Hearne of Penn Street had switched from making chairs to aeroplane parts during a slack period in the late 1930s, thanks to a connection between the Hearnes and aircraft engineer Geoffrey de Havilland, who had been born in Terriers. Parts for the De Havilland 'Mosquito' poured from factories all over the

town—fuselages from Gomme's, wing spars from Dancer & Hearne's out-station at Lindsay Avenue, and veneers from Baker's. The furniture works were ideally suited to making components for the all-wooden Mosquito.

The industrial effects of the war were two-fold. Firstly, there was a profound, colossal, and permanent change in Wycombe's industrial balance. In 1939, 71 per cent of High Wycombe's industrial acreage was devoted to making furniture; engineering occupied 13 per cent and miscellaneous trades (including supplies for the furniture industry), 16 per cent. By 1945, these figures were 35, 29 and 36 per cent respectively. To a degree this was mis-leading because the new engineering firms had far fewer workers per acre compared with the 'hazardous and inconvenient congestion' of the furniture factories, but the signs were clear. Over a third of the furniture factories were officially obsolete and, although Wycombe's staple trade still employed 6,800, its peak had arguably been passed. Businesses amalgamated, and some of the most venerable furniture names were absorbed into super-companies: Gomme's took over Birch's in 1954, for example, and Castle's in 1958. By the late 1950s there were hundreds of students at the College on engineering courses, and the town's biggest employer was Broom & Wade with a 1,400-strong workforce. Like it, the Rye Engineering Company had started out making machines for the chair factories, but had long since diversified. Some former furniture workers deliberately rejected the trade, with its traditions of dirt, short-time working and seasonality, and used experience gained during war service to move into engineering. Whatever Wycombe told itself, it was the 'Furniture Town' no longer.

126 Crowds fill the High Street to hear Winston Churchill endorse the local Conservative candidate from the portico of the *Red Lion* during the post-war election of May 1945.

127 Castle Brothers, the first factory on the Cressex industrial estate, in about 1937: an Art Deco harbinger of a new industrial era.

128 The first premises of Broom & Wade, on waste land behind Lindsay Avenue in 1898.

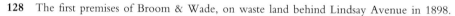

The last of the old-time chair-masters to serve as mayor was William Owen Haines in 1960, and his company was so old-fashioned that it still used the local beechwoods for its chairs. His mayoralty looked like a valediction to the Furniture Town; and Haines's works closed soon afterwards.

Secondly, the war kick-started the local property market in a way which would never really slow again. By the time the conflict was over, Wycombe's population had risen by 4,000,

and makeshift pre-fab expedients would not do to house the new residents permanently. In December 1945 the council revived its pre-war scheme to help house-purchasing, accelerating the drive towards home-ownership ('Why be a tenant? Be your own landlord' the developers' adverts had urged). By 1958 the council had built 2,490 homes and private developers another 1,477. The growth continued until almost the whole of the outline established in the 1930s had been filled in.

129   The factory of Owen Haines & Son, Jubilee Road, in 1960.

130   A perennial and symbolic issue in modern Wycombe is the conflict between the need for housing and the desire to preserve precious green land. This protest against the development of the 'H7' area north-west of Terriers was held in 1972.

131 Bristow & Townsend's furniture factory occupied a site between Copyground Lane and Dashwood Avenue from the 1930s until 1984. The following year, the Bevelwood estate was constructed on the land, a transition typical of many industrial sites in Wycombe.

132 The Pastures, Downley, during the winter of 1977-8. Sands, St Mary & St George's church, and Desborough Castle are in the background. Within ten years this whole hillside would be covered by houses.

The draft 1950 development plan had decided in considerable detail where new housing should go (with the greatest increases in Hazlemere and the Amersham Hill area), but its strictures that Wycombe's skyline should be respected and hilltops not built on soon buckled under the pressure. From the late 1970s the designation of land steeper than a 1:7 gradient as 'white land', unsuitable for housing, was also abandoned, resulting in developments such as the precipitous Imbies estate on the Bellfield. As time went on the search for more space to feed the insatiable demand for housing encompassed former industrial sites (such as the Bevelwood estate built on the site of Bristow & Townsend's chair factory in 1985), allotments (28 houses off Tower Street in Terriers, 1986) and schools (the Lady Verney School estate, 1999). The age of Wycombe's mansion houses reached its last gasp. The big houses at the foot of Amersham Hill were already being converted into flats in the 1930s: twenty years on, and villas such as Desborough House were demolished to make way for blocks. Castle Hill avoided demolition when the Clarkes finally secured the price they wanted and sold it to the borough in 1962; while Fred and Ellen Skull, who had bought the ramshackle Bassetsbury Manor in 1931 and restored it to full Georgian splendour to the delight of *Country*

Life and the like, found that nobody, not even the National Trust, wanted the property, and reluctantly sold it to the council. Terriers House was last lived in during 1950: a plan to convert it to a school failed, and eventually it became the accounts office of Marham's, a London-based tyre manufacturer. Higher domestic and commercial property prices inflated the number of estate agents and concentrated them in one tiny area. The first estate agent in Crendon Street, Hunt & Nash, had moved into no.15 by 1939. By 1952 there were four in Crendon and Easton Streets, rising to six in 1976, 12 by 1988, and 20 by 1999, aided by the surrounding solicitors and surveyors. To suggest that these two streets were now the engine of the whole local economy would be difficult to test, but plausible.

Welsh and Polish incomers would merge into the native townsfolk given time, but the next groups of arrivals were distinguished by more than accents and church-going habits. There had been a handful of black or brown faces in the area for years, especially during the war when black servicemen, both in the US

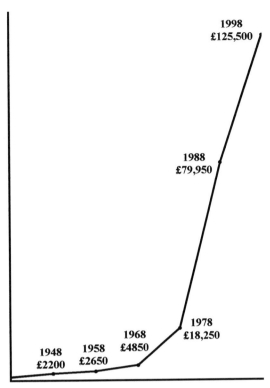

133 The cost of a typical three-bed house on the west side of town, 1948-98.

134 The Maestros and their manager Jennifer Cross, in 1968. The Maestros were a steel band whose members were all St Vincentians living in High Wycombe.

and Imperial forces, became familiar, but large-scale Commonwealth immigration began only later in the 1950s. The largest bodies of immigrants originated from the Caribbean island of St Vincent and the Mirpuri areas of Pakistan, attracted by the promise of jobs and a standard of living unobtainable at home. For most the plan was to spend a few years in Britain sending money home, but changes in immigration laws in the early 1960s encouraged whole families to move in rather than face being split up or permanently excluded.

For most Commonwealth arrivals, the first experience of Britain was one of profound culture shock. West Indians brought up to revere Queen and Empire and to think of Britain as the 'mother country' found themselves in a cold, dreary, unwelcoming environment. Thelma Francis, still thinking Britain was 'paved with gold' approached High Wycombe on the train, seeing 'the smoke coming outta de houses and cloth on de windows' and wondering 'what I leave my beautiful country and come in this place for?' Arshad 'Ash' Chaudhri, son of a high-ranking Kashmiri civil servant, followed his brother to Britain in 1961, disillusioned with the corruption of Pakistan and fuelled by his father's stories of the virtues of the English. Already at Heathrow Airport he was thinking 'we must have been really damn fools, that this nation ruled us for nearly three hundred years', and when his brother took him to the *Nag's Head* on London Road, next to their lodging house, he found not Englishmen in white linen suits and pith helmets, but 'people playing dominoes, all flat caps, with heavy thick hands and fingers and long dirty nails ... I was really shocked, that *these* were the "sahibs"'.

For many new arrivals the first stop in Wycombe was the wartime hostel for migrant workers in Flackwell Heath (there had also been one in Castlefield, but it closed in 1955). It was bought by Wycombe Rural District Council, leased to Broom & Wade to run, and eventually closed in 1970. From the hostel,

immigrants usually moved to a succession of lodging houses, often run by Polish landlords (the only ones who would take them in), where facilities were so restricted that the residents resorted to boiling eggs in kettles and washing in the swimming pool on the Rye where there was 'always a big queue'. As soon as they could, relatives and friends clubbed together to buy houses and gain some independence, usually, though not always, borrowing money from within the family.

This was particularly true for the Asians, who mostly came from poor, illiterate rural areas and who were separated from the native English by language and religion. The story of the first group of Asians in Wycombe shows how this process worked. The first of all (not counting an anonymous man who died on his first night in the Flackwell Heath hostel), Mohammed Hamim Mirza, arrived from London in 1956. The second, Rehmet Ali, was a friend of Mirza's brother and moved into his house in Whitelands Road in 1957. They were soon joined by Hazir Ahmed Butt, a 'friend of a friend' who however quarrelled with Mirza and moved out. Yousif Ali Shah Hashmi got to know this circle through Lol Khan, another of Mirza's lodgers, and later moved in with Rehmet Ali on Perth Road. It was not uncommon to find over twenty men sharing a house, and sleeping at different times. In 1961 the council served 23 notices on overcrowded houses; the inspector expressed irritation at the 'pretence of lack of understanding' which Asian householders used to conceal the truth—although he admitted that very often he was unable to work out whether the person he was talking to was the owner or not.

Wycombe's authorities did tackle the housing issue in more positive ways. Hazir Ahmed Butt was one of hundreds of people who bought a house with a borough council mortgage—185 London Road, in his case; and 1962 saw the establishment of the Wycombe Friendship Housing Association, with the intention of finding accommodation for immi-

135 The impact of the new communities: The Punjab Sweet Centre and East West Food Stores at Temple End photographed in 1978, the site of Mohammed Hamim Mirza's stores of a few years before. These are the same shops as those shown in photograph 84 (p. 74).

136 The stage at the 2001 Asian Mela—the ancient Rye being adapted to a new purpose.

grants. The mayor opened its first dwellings, four flats at 57 Priory Avenue, in 1964. Encouraging the new communities more generally, the inaugural meeting of the Asian Association was attended by the mayor, the council chairman, the police superintendent, the MP's wife Lady Hall, and Col. Harcourt-Powell of the High Commission. The council appointed a Community Liaison Officer in 1967.

Gradually the black and Asian residents became a presence in the town. By the early 1960s the West Indian Cricket Association was playing village teams, and certain churches became heavily West Indian. The Islamic community's search for an appropriate site for a mosque, after other locations had been declared unsuitable, culminated in 1981 when a foundation stone was laid in Jubilee Road. Asian food needs began to be addressed when Mohammed Hamim Mirza began a delivery business in 1962, serving customers as far afield as Banbury, before he opened specialist stores

137 An early Asian presence in Wycombe, though more a migrant than an immigrant: a Sikh carpet-seller at the Market, 1933, captured in a newspaper photo-collage.

at 55 Dashwood Avenue and Temple End. Caribbean Carnivals, beginning in Castlefield, and the Asian Mela on the Rye, became features in Wycombe's cultural calendar from 1982 and 1996 respectively. The new situation was recognised when Mohammed Razzaq became mayor in 1988, followed by Sebert Graham in 1996, the first from the Pakistani and St Vincentian communities to hold that office. A more unusual first was scored when local West Indians helped Alston Nedd and his wife Jean to purchase the licence of the *Bird-At-Hand* on West Wycombe Road in 1968, the first black husband-and-wife publicans in Britain. After Alston's death, Jean became Britain's first black sole landlady. The Cultural Resources Centre was started in the Council's Multi-Racial Centre off Paul's Row in 1985 to campaign on issues such as getting Asian

food served in the hospital. The change in the nature of the town was most obvious in the old Victorian terraced streets where Asian residents, and Asian food, clothing and amenity stores became concentrated. In Jubilee Road, for instance, the first Asian to appear on the electoral register moved in during 1961. There were still only six in 1970, but numbers then rose quickly to 53 in 1985 and 65 in 2000—almost three-quarters of the street's 89 voters.

But the absorption of Wycombe's new citizens was not without its problems. Canny employers such as Long & Hambly looked at the immigrants' willingness to work long hours for little pay, and then at the balance sheet, and signed them up in dozens. But for every immigrant offered three jobs in one day, as some claimed they were, there were many others who suspected, and were occasionally told outright, that employers were rejecting them for their skin colour. Already by 1962 white residents were expressing 'disgust' at efforts to house immigrants, and this resentment would turn uglier with time. In the late 1970s there was an upsurge in racist activity. White children chanted 'Enoch Powell' at their black schoolmates in playgrounds; the offices of the Wycombe Council for Racial Equality were repeatedly vandalised; the National Front marched through the town in 1978 and fought with the Anti-Nazi League; and the NF candidate secured over 2,000 votes in that year's Wycombe by-election. In 1979 Mr Bell, the MP for Beaconsfield, spoke of immigrants 'swamping' Britain and said they should be paid £2,000 to return 'home'. Ash Chaudhri, a former policeman and a community activist, organised a protest march, beginning in Frogmoor and culminating in an offer of £4,000 to the MP to leave the country! Even without political agitation, tension was just below the surface. At five to two on New Year's morning, 1988, an argument between a black youth and two whites outside the Multi-Racial Centre ended in an attack on the *Anchor* pub, Keen's photographers being looted, and

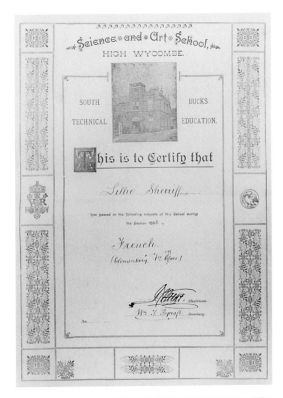

138 Lillie Sherriff's certificate for achievements in French, awarded by the School of Science & Art, as it then was, in 1896.

139 Desborough Street children's playground, 1976, with Green Street School (founded 1896 and now closed) in the background.

26 arrests. This brawl, grandly called a 'riot', provoked much soul-searching in the town. There were also divisions between the non-white communities, and the Council for Racial Equality was repeatedly disrupted by allegations of bias and vote-rigging according to whether its Asian or West Indian members had lost its elections, until the exasperated district council finally pulled the plug on the organisation in 1994.

One final factor brought a significant change to Wycombe: the growth of the college. The foundation stone of the School of Science and Art was laid in Frogmoor in 1893; most of the establishment moved in 1919 into the old Grammar School buildings on Easton Street, and then in the 1950s to a purpose-built modernist block on Queen Alexandra Road. In 1939 there were nine full-time lecturers; in 1954, about sixty. The new building was described by its principal, W.J. Davies, as 'something entirely new, in accommodation, equipment and everything else'. The college continued growing until its acquisition of university status in 1999. The sites of the little Victorian terraces of Brook Street were turned into a student hall of residence, and the *Saracen's Head* in Green Street, for many years a popular Afro-Caribbean pub, closed in 1999 and was converted into 20-odd student rooms. In the late 1990s hardly a week went by without the council receiving applications to convert houses into multi-occupancy. In the 1960s this would have meant immigrants, but thirty years later it showed that students were moving, mainly, into old houses in the run-down parts of the town which the former immigrant communities were now leaving. To an extent, the introduction of student tuition fees put this process into reverse as young people became unable to afford to live away from home, and by 2001 the 'foreign' proportion of the university's 9,000 core students was down to a quarter.

The Wycombe into which these students were moving was a very different town from its incarnation of sixty years before. Its tradi-tional industries were now of relatively minor importance. Although the area's furniture makers raised a Chair Arch in the time-honoured position beside the Guildhall to celebrate the Millennium, the old staple trade employed only a fraction of the numbers it once had, with the closure of companies such as Glenister's and its replacement by a Safeway's store, and the departure of the biggest firms to cheaper areas—Parker-Knoll's factory to Chipping Norton in 1988, and Gomme's to Melksham and Glasgow in 1993. Even Ercol, the most self-consciously traditionalist of the big manufacturers, was unable to expand or rebuild on its hemmed-in site, and by the mid-1990s was looking for a new home. There might be hundreds of students on the college's design courses, but only a handful entered local furniture firms each year. Paper, the other old industry, had become concentrated in fewer and fewer sites. When Marsh Mill announced its closure in 1992, the *Free Press* described the decision with gloomy lyricism—'the heart of High Wycombe's paper industry would gradually slow down, and then stop beating forever'. Glory Mill at Wooburn, the last paper-maker on the Wye, was closed by its German owners Bunzl in 1999.

Other changes were less obvious, but just as profound. In 1936, Mayor Roland Clarke declared 'one of my greatest fears is that we will become suburbanised. I want Wycombe, forever if possible, to maintain its position as an old country market town.' It had long since ceased to be that even as the words passed his lips, but it was still parochial enough for the girls at the telephone switchboard to have to be 'experts in understanding the Bucks dialect'. Yet the next six decades would be a continuing story of loss of independence and erosion of distinctiveness, a story which could of course be told by many towns. Under the impact of war, in 1942 the borough's volunteer fire brigade was absorbed within the National Fire Service. The borough police force and its schools were next, merging with the county's

140 The Millennium Chair Arch, 2000.

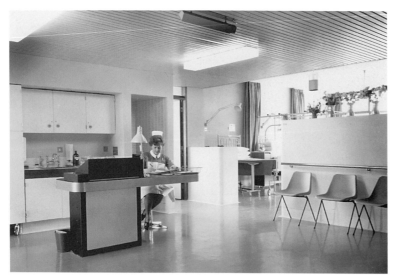

141 A ward at the new hospital building, 1966.

142 The waterworks staff in 1960, just before the County Council took it over.

143 Change and continuity: at various times, these early 1900s factory buildings at 35 Queens Road housed the chair firms of Stone's, Pixton's, and Nicholls & Janes—the last left after 1968. The buildings were then occupied by many small ventures from design companies to a performance studio and a fancy-dress hire business, and are currently due for demolition.

144 The Swan Theatre, opened in 1992, entirely changed the southern approaches to the town as well as providing an arts venue.

in 1946; then the hospital, which despite record public contributions was in the red year after year, had to succumb to the National Health Service in 1948. 'We surrender our trust', warned the board's chairman Percy Raffety at its last meeting, 'not from our own volition, but under compulsion.' Wycombe lost control of its water supply to the county council in 1960. Finally, the movement for the reorganisation of local government resulted in the amalgamation of the Borough Council with Wycombe Rural and Marlow Urban District Councils: as a consequence even the library

followed the other institutions into the county's hands. The new Wycombe District Council, which first met in 1973, rejected constitution as a borough in deference to the feelings of Marlow and the villages: they were already resentful at being 'taken over' by their big neighbour and would have resented a new mayor based there even more. Instead the mayor of High Wycombe would in future be elected by the Charter Trustees, the councillors representing the old borough wards; they became the guardians of its traditions, regalia and ceremonies, which were now free-floating

145 *Left.* A 1935 advert for Murray's, 'the new walk-round store', another reason for outsiders to visit High Wycombe.

146 *Above.* Dring's the outfitters occupied the old *Chequers Inn* at 3 Church Street between about 1867 and the mid-1950s. By the 1970s this medieval building had fallen into extreme disrepair (locals joked that it was only held up by its covering of illegal posters) and, despite a campaign to save it, it was demolished in 1981. The two men may be Walter Birch and Arthur Vernon.

picturesque antiquities completely disconnected from the governance of the town.

Little was actually *made* in the town centre any more (the last chair-maker there, Nicholls & Janes, moved out in 1958 to make way for a new college building), and less was bought and sold too—or, at least, fewer varieties of things. The Octagon had been the council's attempt to turn Wycombe into a regional shopping centre, but it seemed to have failed. In 1981 a High Wycombe Society survey found most people critical both of it and the shops in general: people went to Slough, Reading, Oxford or even Marlow for anything out of the ordinary. The tale of the town's department stores was instructive. After McIlroy's closed in 1953 its site was sold to Marks & Spencer, but its place in Wycombe's commercial life was taken by Murray's. This store was founded by Reginald Rivett in 1923 when he bought the drapery department of Dring's and Frank Adams's sports shop above it; it was named

after Mr Rivett's young son. Murray's marketed itself as 'the new walk-round store' in contrast to the old-fashioned McIlroy's where goods were not on open display, and expanded its White Hart Street site in 1957, trumpeted as 'Buckinghamshire's most modern store' and boasting its own café. It began to suffer in the early-'80s recession, contracted, and eventually closed in 1985. Its replacement was not a town centre store at all, but the first non-metropolitan branch of John Lewis, which opened at Handy Cross the following year. The development of Handy Cross had begun with the building of the sports centre in 1975; the *Crest Hotel* arrived there in 1982, meeting a need which Wycombe's businesses had been complaining about for years, and a new cinema followed in 1987. 'A cinema like no other', claimed the publicity; but the point was rather that it was, or would soon be, exactly like every other, part of a national chain like the hotel and the store. The area was now a second centre of

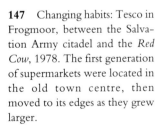

147 Changing habits: Tesco in Frogmoor, between the Salvation Army citadel and the *Red Cow*, 1978. The first generation of supermarkets were located in the old town centre, then moved to its edges as they grew larger.

148   The development of Handy Cross began in 1975 with the Sports Centre, the successor to Aleck Stacey's town centre swimming baths.

balance for Wycombe, containing all those facilities which could not fit into the old town as their smaller forebears had. Indeed, for thousands of car-bound visitors Handy Cross, with the M40 close at hand and ample space for parking, *was* High Wycombe, not the ancient borough on the valley floor.

Yet although local people looked back nostalgically to what they thought was Wycombe's golden age, the changes obscured the fact that the town was simply doing what it had done since the Middle Ages—ditching the past and moving on with unsentimental but productive entrepreneurship. Pharmaceutical manufacturing, electronics and, increasingly, banking and financial services were becoming part of the economic bedrock. Between 1981 and 1997 the proportion of the population employed by manufacturing almost halved, but employment in the financial sector

shot up from eight per cent to 26 per cent—and even then manufacturing was still above the national average. For the new companies, Wycombe's traditional advantage of proximity to London, now speedily reached along the M40 rather than the old road, was as important as ever. Typical was the American instruments manufacturer Instron, which moved its British HQ to the Cressex industrial estate in 1961 in anticipation of the motorway. But the majority of companies were small—in 1997, 94 per cent, in fact, had fewer than twenty workers, yet again repeating the town's traditional pattern. Like the furniture firms of old, for instance, the electronics manufacturer Beta Instruments was founded by two friends in a shed in 1967; it moved first to the Vernon Building and then Cressex, and by the 1990s exported 90 per cent of its output and employed 85 people.

Per capita income remained high and unemployment generally low. High Wycombe's businesses made it the seventh most profitable town in the country according to one 2000 survey. Prosperity helps to explain why a town with a non-white population nudging a quarter of the total had never suffered from significant racial strife—the 'riot' of 1988 was a petty affair compared with the disturbances of the early 1900s—and even Wycombe's 'problem' areas were not that *much* of a problem. The estates

created in the 1930s, Castlefield and Micklefield, had by the 1970s indeed acquired a reputation for vandalism and deprivation. 'A public lavatory in a city slum area?', the *Free Press* sardonically captioned a photograph of an apparently derelict building in 1978, 'No, this is Castlefield Branch Library in one of its better moments'. At various times Wycombe's bus drivers refused to go into either area after dark. Yet these were districts which could run community centres and organise carnivals, and where unemployment,

149 The *Red Lion* statue is manoeuvred gingerly from the ground floor to the first floor of Wycombe Museum in 1995. This unofficial symbol of Wycombe, erected on a portico outside the *Red Lion Hotel* in the High Street in the 1820s, was replaced in 1956, and the original travelled to Hughenden Manor before coming to the Museum in 1985.

150 In 1962 Queen Elizabeth II paid an official visit to High Wycombe, and was shown round a reconstructed wood-turner's hut, assembled in the Town Hall. Here, librarian and museum curator John Mayes conducts the Queen around the display. Wycombe still defined itself by the furniture industry, even though other trades were already more important.

albeit up to three times what it was over the valley in Downley, was still running at less than 3½ per cent in 1999. The fact that Wycombe people could talk about Castlefield and Micklefield in the same breath as Moss Side and St Paul's said more about Wycombe in general than it did about the estates.

———◦◦◦◦———

'You'll think this is an odd thing to say', warned the visitor to the Museum, 'But I've always felt that High Wycombe has a touch of the Wild West about it!' Odd it may have sounded, and it may have been more true at some times than others (especially during the hectic, uncontrolled changes of the 19th century), but this statement provides a key to understanding the town's whole history. It is what unites the Roman farmers, the traders of the medieval borough, and the corn factors struggling against the market regulations; the paper entrepreneurs, the rough-and-ready chair-masters, the Asian shopkeepers and the founders of computer companies. Powered by its river and its road, fuelled by the huge market of London at the other end of that road, Wycombe has never been a soft-edged place, but one where fortunes are made and lost. Beneath the comings and goings of industries and people, behind the shifting boundaries of the town's outline, the deep engines of its history motor on. High Wycombe's future will surely follow the same pattern as its past.

Appendix: Watercress growing on the Wye

One minor Wycombe trade about which little is known, but which touches on the history of the river, is watercress growing. The first known reference to Wycombe watercress comes in Kingston's *History* of 1848, when it was supposedly 'a comparatively modern source of employment amongst a great number of industrious families'. 'Hereabouts the industrious cresser may be seen, stalking heedlessly in his jack-boots … with the addition of his striped jersey, he … dexterously plucks his emerald crop'.

This account appears to be exaggerated, since there are very few references to people actually earning their living in the watercress business. Nonetheless, the presence of a 'watercress cultivator' and five 'watercressmen' in 1851 implies quite a significant trade. All of them lived on or around West Wycombe Road where the majority of the beds were, and all but one were members of the Weedon and Pepall families. However by 1875 there was only one full-time cress worker. There were still at least six sets of cress beds along the Wye in the 1920s, possibly managed by the Putnams, the family most strongly associated with the cress trade in later times. Most of the details seem to have died out of local memory, though, and the Putnams only occasionally bothered to advertise in the trade directories.

If Kingston's account is at all trustworthy, he may have been remembering the situation some years before his book was published, and the 1851 census return therefore shows us a business in decline. Alternatively, cress-gathering was perhaps a side-line resorted to when other trade was slack, in the same way that the chair workers went to Flackwell Heath and other villages to pick cherries in the summer. This would explain why cress workers hardly ever appear in official records. It does not explain, however, why cress-gathering seems never to have cropped up in the recorded memories of Wycombe people in the way that cherry-picking has.

Bibliography

Ashford, L.J., *History of the Borough of High Wycombe* (1960)

Bland, S., *Parker Knoll* (1989)

Bucks WIs, *Bucks Within Living Memory* (1993)

Burgin, M., *The Women's Suffrage Movement in High Wycombe* (c.1998)

Carter, S., *A Recorded History of Compair Broomwade* (1998)

Cauvain, S. and P., 'A Romano-British Site at Micklefield, High Wycombe', *Records of Bucks* 20 (1978)

Chaudhri, A., *Home to Home* (1988)

Chepping Wycombe Parish Council, *Portrait of a Parish* (2000)

Chitty, A.M., *Advisory Development Plan for High Wycombe & District* (1950)

Cleaver, A., *Strange Wycombe* (1986)

Collard, M., 'Excavations at Desborough Castle', *Records of Bucks* 30 (1988)

Cotton, B.D., *The English Regional Chair* (1990)

Denton, E., 'Lives of the Newland Chairmakers', Oxford University thesis (1995)

Dimocke, H., ed., *Magna Vita Sancti Hugonis* (1864)

Dixon, P.H., 'Breweries, Pubs and the Temperance Society in High Wycombe', Oxford BA thesis

Edmunds, T., *Church & Community in Terriers* (2000)

Etherington, E., *A History of Further Education in High Wycombe* (1969)

Finch, D. and Peart, S., *Wycombe Wanderers: The Official History* (1997)

Flint, L., *Wycombe Abbey School: A Partial History* (1989)

Garmondsway, G.W., ed., *The Anglo-Saxon Chronicle* (1972)

Gibbs, R., *Bucks Miscellany* (1891)

Gladstone, C., *Totteridge* (2000)

Greaves, R.W., ed., *First Ledger Book of High Wycombe* (1955)

Green, H., *The Parish Church of High Wycombe* (1964)

Green, H., *100 Years of Education* (1970)

Grinsey, L., *Davenport Vernon: a Celebration* (1986)

Harbour, H., *The Homeland Handbooks* (1909)

Hartley, B., 'A Romano-British Villa at High Wycombe', *Records of Bucks* 16 (1959)

Hepple, Leslie W. and Doggett, Alison M., *The Chilterns* (1992)

Howland, P., 'A History of Wycombe Borough Police', University of Birmingham thesis (c.1955)

Hume, B., ed., *A Victorian Engagement* (1975)

Janes, R.A., 'Wycombe Memories', *Cabinet Maker & Complete House Furnisher* (4.8.1951)

Judson, W., *High Wycombe Directory* (1875)

Kalina, W., *Winnie's Wycombe* (c.1990)

Kingston, H., *History of Wycombe* (1848)

Langley, T., *History of the Hundred of Desborough* (1797)

Leaver, R., *Naphill, a Village in Perspective* (1999)

Le Hardy, W., ed., *Calendar to the Bucks Session Records* (1933-39)

MacDermott, E.T., *History of the Great Western Railway* (1964)

McMillan, M., *The Black Boy Pub and Other Stories* (1997)

Mawer, A. and Stenton, F.M., *Place Names of Buckinghamshire* (1925)

Mayes, L.J., *The History of Chairmaking in High Wycombe* (1960)

Mayes, L.J., *A History of the Borough of High Wycombe from 1880* (1960)

Mayes, L.J., 'Some Customs in the Chairmaking Trade—2', *The Woodworker*, October 1960

Mayes, L.J., *Paper in the Wye Valley* (1976)

Mead, A., *Days of Glory* (1999)

Parker, J., *History & Antiquities of High Wycombe* (1878)

Pearce, O., *Wycombe Rebel* (1982)

Pearce, O., *A Family History* (1980)

Pevsner, N. and Williamson, E., *The Buildings of England: Buckinghamshire* (1993)

Rattani, A., ed., *Wycombe Is Something Else* (1989)

Reed, M., *A History of Buckinghamshire* (1993)

Roden, D., in *Forestry*, vol. 41 no.1 (1968)

Roussell, T., *Downley in Times Past* (1983)

Scruton, J., *The Rye, A Priceless Possession* (1976)

Scruton, O. and Alexander, F., *Jack Scruton* (1991)

Sheahan, J.J., *History & Topography of Buckinghamshire* (1862)

Sparkes, I.G., *The English Country Chair* (1973)

Sparkes, I.G., *The Book of Wycombe* (1979)

Sparkes, I.G., *High Wycombe: A Pictorial History* (1990)

Summers, W.H., 'Some Documents in the State Papers relating to High Wycombe', *Records of Bucks* 7 (1895)

Sutcliffe, B.P. and Church, D.C., *250 Years of Chiltern Methodism* (1988)

Tapsell, M., *Memories of Bucks Picture Palaces* (1983)

Taylor, D.W., *Terriers House, a Brief History* (n.d.)

Travers, A., ed., *Bucks Feet of Fines 1259-1307* (1989)

Tyer, G. and Abbott, C.W., *High Wycombe, its Resources & Advantages* (1894)

Uttley, A., *Buckinghamshire* (1950)

Veysey, J., *The Ongoing Story of a Church* (1995)

Veysey, J., *Hughenden Valley* (2000)

Watt, J., *Granny Loosley's Kitchen Album* (1980)

Wycombe Museum, *A Brief History of Wycombe Pubs* (1998)

Index